WHEN

MY PARENTS

WERE MY AGE,

THEY WERE OLD

· · · · · OR · · · · ·

Who Are You Calling

Middle-Aged?

by Cathy Crimmins

A Fireside Book
Published by Simon & Schuster
New York   London   Toronto   Sydney   Tokyo   Singapore

FIRESIDE
Rockefeller Center
1230 Avenue of the Americas
New York, NY 10020

Designed by Liney Li

Manufactured in the United States of America

10   9   8   7   6   5   4   3   2   1

Library of Congress Cataloging-in-Publication Data

Crimmins, C. E.
When my parents were my age, they were old, or Who are yc
calling middle-aged? / by Cathy Crimmins.
p.   cm.
"A Fireside book."
1. Baby-boom generation—United States—Humor.   2. Middle
United States—Humor.   I. Title.   II. Title: Who are you calling mi(
HQ1059.5.U5C75   1995
305.24'4'0973—dc20   94-45941
CIP
ISBN: 0-684-80289-9

FOR JOHN GAGGIN

ACKNOWLEDGMENTS*

Thanks to my fellow midketeers for sharing angst and laughs: Susan Albertine, Lisa Bankoff, Louise Berliner, George Bilyk, Barbara Blake, Jackie Buhn, Betsy Caesar, Sandy Caesar, Debbie Crimmins, Dorothy Daub, Cecelia Denegre, David Diamond, Kay Dowgun, Marion Frank, Terry Gillen, Paul Goerss, Jay Grossman, Susan Harris, Jovida Hill, Sue Huntington, Steve Huntington, Rick Johansen, Diane Kalin, Margo Kaufman, Martin Kenney, Gerald Kolpan, Mark Kramer, Nick Kulish, Laura McMunigal, Angela McNally, Barry Mike, Michael Pedretti, Nick Proffitt, Alan Razak, Flash Rosenberg, Steve Ross, Diane Schaefer, Jim Schank, Cat Thompson, Margaret Tobin, Jane Von Bergen, Janice Walker, Roz Warren, Deb Werksman, Taylor Williams, Jon Winokur, Ben Yagoda, and Hans Zarbock.

Eliot Kaplan at *Philadelphia Magazine* was very sensitive to the

*Some of the people I am acknowledging here have requested this disclaimer: Just because we helped you with this book and our names are in it does *not* mean that we are middle-aged in any way.

material in its first form, and someday I might even forgive him for being a year younger than I am. I also want to thank close humorists Tom O'Leary, Peter Hoelter, Robin Warshaw, Frank Costello, St. James Shatzer, and Richard Dowgun, for lending me terrific quips and yarns. As always, I'm grateful to Joanne Babaian, Sarah Babaian, and Joellen Brown, who provide the spandex for my sagging soul.

Tom Maeder, whose mind is even sicker than mine, contributed generously to the listing of future boomer products and to many other sections. I can't thank him enough for his enthusiasm, but I *can* offer him all patent rights to the bifocal windshield. Bruce Schimmel and Kate Maskar, directors of the Brayke Wynds Foundation in historic Milton, Delaware, were extremely helpful, providing the solitude necessary to finish the manuscript.

I'm grateful to Betty Kelly for making me part of the baby boom, and to Marilyn Abraham, who followed my career until I was old enough to have her as my editor. Finally, I'd like to acknowledge all sorts of assistance provided by my daughter, Kelly, and my husband, Alan Forman, who help me find nearly everything I lose, including (sometimes) my sense of humor.

CONTENTS

Part Two: The Body Politic: Health, Fitness, and Sex   27

Part Three: The Days of Our Lifestyles . . . Food, Clothing, Shelter, and Entertainment   53

Part Four: Grown-up Stuff:
Time, Memory, Money, Work, Etc. 95

Part Five: Hope I Die Before I Get Old (Not!) 115

A Note on the Typeface

This is the type size we were going to use,
but the author and her friends found themselves
squinting,
so we decided to use

RELAXED-FIT TYPE.

Better, huh?

Breathe deeply and enjoy the book.

PART ONE

Welcome to the Relaxed-Fit Years,

or

What, Me— Middle-Aged?

Something's happening here.

- My jeans are shrinking.
- The president of the United States is young enough to be my husband.
- I need reading glasses.
- My thighs are falling.
- Trolls are back.

I never expected to live past thirty, and now I've shot past thirty-something right into the great unknown middlesomething.

How can this be happening to me? And, please, I need to know:

AM I EVER GOING TO BE AS DORKY AS MY PARENTS WERE WHEN THEY WERE MIDDLE-AGED?

No? You really mean it? Thanks. That's the way I feel about you, too. None of us can be that dorky, ever, because we're part of the hippest generation that ever lived. Time is on our side. We were born during an incredible wrinkle in history, when anything was possible, and it still is. Sure, we're getting a little older. But that doesn't mean we've turned into June and Ward Cleaver. We're still cool. We're still the biggest generation of rebels that this world has ever seen.

We invented sex.
We invented drugs.
We invented rock and roll.
The next step for us boomers?

WE WILL INVENT A NEW MIDDLE AGE

Sure, why not? There are 76 million of us, and if we say **HELL, NO, WE WON'T GO,** we won't. Who says we have to plunge into the midlife doldrums like our folks did? We're much better prepared. We've got stair-climbing machines, Retin-A, and spandex. Most importantly, we've got **ATTITUDE.** (Sure, our parents and the Generation X people behind us might prefer to call it "denial," but that's just sour grapes.)

So let's begin deconstructing this traditional middle-age myth right now. If you're special, like we are, you never have to be *really* middle-aged, driving big cars and buying the Mrs. a mink and cooking tuna casseroles and actually liking Lawrence Welk and talking about the weather and falling asleep in a Barca-Lounger with your mouth open and wearing ugly eyeglasses on a string around your neck.

Of course, we do drive minivans and buy our beloveds shearling coats and cook pasta and listen to Harry Connick Jr. and occasionally watch the Weather Channel. But hardly any of us fall asleep in front of Letterman since he moved up an hour. And some of us do wear glasses around our necks, but they're designer glasses with neon strings or handwoven attachments made by natives, and part of the money goes to save the rain forest.

So, it's clear: we're different. These years ahead of us are going to be a *truly unique experience,* much cooler than anything our parents ever went through. This is not your father's Oldsmobile. This is a vibrant, fulfilling, hip time of life for us. Call it New Middle Age. Or, if you cringe at the mention of *middle* and *age* together in one sentence, call this time ahead of us the Relaxed-Fit Years. Whatever you dub them, these are the crowning years of our mature young adulthood. The attitude? I'm stuck in the middle with you, and I plan to have a hell of a lot of fun while I'm here.

Checklist: Signs That You Might Be Halfway Up That Stairway to Heaven

✓ You've started musing about the shallow value system of people in their twenties.

✓ You tune in more often to the local news than to MTV.

✓ You wince when the scanner hits a rap station.

✓ You find yourself telling your babysitter about your first boyfriend/girlfriend.

✓ Many of the doctors in hospitals look like Doogie Howser to you.

✓ You suddenly desperately need your first reading glasses, crown, arthroscopic surgery, extramarital affair, Armani suit, elastic waistband, fiber-laden cereal, sportscar, baby, inheritance, root canal, dye job, hotel getaway . . .

✓ You truly enjoy the Disney Channel specials featuring ancient rock stars of the past who look—hey!—pretty good.

✓ There are house repairs you've been meaning to do for over a decade.

✓ You know the difference between Sinéad O'Connor and Sandra Day O'Connor.

✓ All of the professional athletes you admire are at least ten year younger than you.

✓ You no longer care as much if you don't go out on Sunda night.

✓ You yearn more wistfully for former repairmen than for cer tain ex-lovers.

✓ You've begun to go toward the *lite*—lite beer, lite rock, lit butter, lite literature . . .

✓ You are too old for Doc Martens, but too young for Do Kevorkian.

Don't Trust Anyone over Sixty: Once Classic Symptoms of Encroaching Maturity and How Our Generation Has Rehabbed Them

Just like those cute townhouses we renovated in the seventies and eighties, Middle Age has become a focus for gentrification.
Now that our generation's gotten our hands on it, it will never seem boring again.

OLD MIDDLE AGE (our parents)	*New Middle Age* (*us*)
Your mind starts wandering and you begin telling long-winded stories about your youth or about every little thing you did on your vacation.	Your mind starts wandering and you dub yourself a monologuist. They book you into Lincoln Center or a Broadway theater for fifty bucks a head to tell long, rambling stories about yourself. Living proof: Spalding Gray, Wallace Shawn, Eric Bogosian, Karen Finley, and Lily Tomlin.
You start to go gray so you dye your hair.	You begin highlighting your hair to enhance its natural shine.
You start not to be able to eat certain foods because they give you gas.	Your nutritional advisor gives you a strict diet to follow to maximize your energy.
Your knees start to go.	You undergo arthroscopic surgery and a therapy regimen at a sports medicine facility.
You begin to drink a little too much and tell embarrassing stories at parties.	You stop drinking and write embarrassing essays or books about how awful you were when you were drinking.

When Does the
Pepsi Generation Lose Its Fizz?
A Meditation

● ● ●

How many inner children can hip-hop on the end of a pin?
When does middle age begin, if ever?

Attitudinal Adjustment Approach

This is a young society, getting younger all the time. Adolescence
which used to end at eighteen, has been extended to age twenty-
five. Young adulthood now runs from twenty-five to fifty, and
mature young adulthood goes from fifty to seventy. In this model
one needn't worry about being classically middle-aged until after
seventy.

Historical/Demographic Approach

As humankind's life span increases due to advances in health and
technology, so does the age of midlife onset. In Charlemagne's
time, fifteen-year-olds were middle-aged, and no one had to
budget for expensive dental work because most people were dead
before age thirty-five. Today, with a woman's average life span of
seventy-eight, she reaches her midlife point a scant year before
going through the ordeal of her surprise fortieth birthday party.
Ah, progress!

Philosophical Approach

There is no such thing as middle age. The true "middle" of your
life can only be pondered by future generations. Say you are forty-
two and walk in front of a bus tomorrow. Unbeknownst to you,
your middle years had already commenced at twenty-one. (If you
were even subliminally experiencing a midlife crisis at twenty-
one, it might account for that bad acid trip you had back then.)

Mommy Nearest

I finally had to accept that I was getting a little older when all my favorite actresses, the ones who are my age, started playing maternal roles. Bette Midler, Jessica Lange, Cher — all somebody's _mother?_ And I'm not talking toddlers, either. They're playing people with _grown_ children. Those are roles that are supposed to be acted by Geraldine Page and Colleen Dewhurst. Being dead is no excuse! Those older actresses are supposed to play the mothers _forever._

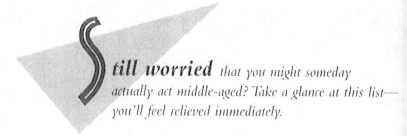

Still worried that you might someday actually act middle-aged? Take a glance at this list—you'll feel relieved immediately.

Hell, No—We Won't Go . . .
People Who Were Born Old (Not Like Us)

Eleanor Roosevelt	Spiro Agnew	Uncle Fester
Queen Elizabeth	Leona Helmsley	Edward Hermann
Winston Churchill	Mr. Ed	Joan Rivers
Charlie Weaver	Rush Limbaugh	Betty Crocker
Dr. Joyce Brothers	Julia Child	Golda Meir
Al Gore	Mister Rogers	Dan and Marilyn Quayle
Nancy Reagan	Zsa Zsa Gabor	Aunt Jemima
Groucho Marx	Wayne Newton	Margaret Dumont
Walter Brennan	W. C. Fields	Jon Lovitz
Maggie Smith	Phyllis Diller	Josephine the Plumber
Jackie Gleason	Daniel Moynihan	
Aunt Bea	Donald Duck	Sigmund Freud
Henry Morgan	Dagwood Bumstead	Bob Hope

Aging Boomer
Gods and Goddesses:

THE
NEW PANTHEON

•

Boomer Goddesses:

Hillary Clinton, Susan Sarandon,
Martha Stewart, Bette Midler, Diane Sawyer,
Roseanne, Jane Pauley,
Candice Bergen, Barbra Streisand,
Linda Ronstadt, Meryl Streep, Lauren Hutton,
Goldie Hawn, Jane Fonda, Connie Chung,
Katie Couric, Bonnie Raitt, Anne Rice,
Joni Mitchell, Judy Collins, Susan Powter,
Richard Simmons

Boomer Gods:

Bill Clinton, Eric Clapton, Stephen King,
Steven Spielberg, Billy Joel, Bruce Springsteen,
Harrison Ford, Neil Young, Kevin Costner,
Bill Murray, Nolan Ryan, Paul McCartney,
Mick Jagger, Jimmy Connors, Howard Stern,
David Letterman, William Gates, k.d. lang

Celebrity Activities for This Awkward Phase

Time stops for no man or woman, even those with the resources to give it a run for its money. How, exactly, do the more famous among us manifest the signs of New Middle Age?

- Performing duets with dead parents
- Losing fifty or sixty pounds
- Shopping for plastic surgeons
- Making out at baseball games with third millionaire husband
- Inventing new perfumes
- Opening restaurants
- Wearing dorky eyeglasses to movie openings to look intelligent
- Making public announcements about how you're still trying to have a baby at the age of forty-seven
- Filming infomercials for skin-care products
- Dating girlfriend's daughter
- Walking around without a toupee to show you're a cool guy
- Having change-of-life babies
- Going on *Oprah* to plug book about your past drug use, alcoholism, or childhood sexual abuse

Ask Miss Denial

Q I went to a concert with some friends, and the guy in the warm-up act did a really fantastic set of Van Morrison songs. He sounded *so much* like him, but he was really old and fat and balding. Afterward someone said it *was* Van Morrison. I don't believe it, do you?

A Of course not. It's amazing how many rock star impersonators just don't bother to keep up their appearances.

Q The afternoon of my twentieth high school reunion, I decided to attend my alma mater's football game. On the team was a sixteen-year-old kid who looked exactly like one of my friends and had the same last name. I thought it must be Butch's little brother. But then later someone at the reunion dance told me it was Butch's *son*. I don't believe it, do you?

A Of course not. Butch would have been some sort of pervert to have sired a kid at twenty-two, which is probably why you were too embarrassed to ask him about it personally. No, there has to be some other explanation. I recommend doing a genealogical search for cousins.

Q Help! I am getting really fat. Is this going to last forever?

A Of course not. What you're noticing is just baby boomer fat. Don't worry, you'll outgrow it.

From Hipsters to Midsters:

What a difference two decades make. Baby boomers have passed from the larval hippie stage of life through the transitional yuppie ectomorph phase, only to arrive at the New Middle Age.

DRUG OF CHOICE

'70s: marijuana

'80s: cocaine

'90s: Prozac

RULING FORCES

'70s: sex

'80s: money

'90s: gravity

VACATION ACTIVITY

'70s: bumming around Europe

'80s: trekking in Himalayas

'90s: standing in line at Space Mountain

PERFECT PICKUP

'70s: bed partner

'80s: Szechuan

'90s: kids from summer camp

PORTENTS CONSULTED DAILY

'70s: tarot cards

'80s: stock market listings

'90s: bathroom scale

ALBUMS

'70s: Beatles' *White Album*

'80s: Simon's *Graceland*

'90s: Disney's soundtrack of *Beauty and the Beast*

SEX GURUS

'70s: Alex Comfort

'80s: Dr. Ruth

'90s: C. Everett Koop

PROPHETIC LITERATURE

'70s: *FutureShock* (Toffler)

'80s: *Megatrends* (Naisbitt)

'90s: *Final Exit* (Humphries)

How Did We Get Here So Fast?

FLANNEL SHIRT

'70s: army surplus store

'80s: L.L. Bean

'90s: grunge boutique

NAVEL-GAZING LITERATURE

'70s: Carlos Castaneda

'80s: *Passages*

'90s: *Everything I Need to Know, I Learned in Kindergarten*

RITE OF PASSAGE TO YAK ABOUT

'70s: Woodstock

'80s: EST

'90s: twentieth high school reunion

CINEMATIC EXPERIENCE

'70s: *Easy Rider*

'80s: *Big Chill*

'90s: *The Lion King*

MALE GURUS

'70s: Timothy Leary

'80s: Michael Milken

'90s: John Bradshaw

DISCUSSION TOPIC

'70s: generation gap

'80s: gender gap

'90s: Gap ads

TRENDY ILLNESS

'70s: mono

'80s: chronic fatigue syndrome

'90s: Lyme disease

FAVORITE TELEVISION SHOW

'70s: *Star Trek*

'80s: *Star Trek: The Next Generation*

'90s: *Star Trek: Deep Space Nine*

FUNGI

'70s: psychedelic mushrooms

'80s: shiitakes

'90s: athlete's foot

The Boomer Achievement Test (BAT): Take the Test of Time

How many standardized tests have you endure in your lifetime? Ironic, isn't it, that the least standard generatio in history was forced on a nearly daily basis to take out our num ber two pencils and fill in little dots?

Well, here's a user-friendly quiz determining *not* how star dard you are but how truly unique your achievements have bee to date. The Educational Testing Service will never touch th test, and neither your children nor your parents will ever see you score. Anyone who has made it this far will score well, reflectir that individual spark we've all come to know and love.

1. Of the items on the following list, please check off an that you now have opinions about that you probabl didn't twenty years ago.

___gas barbecues   ___floor coverings
___chiropractors   ___olive oil
___ex-spouses   ___pensions

IDDLE AGE·GREAT MOMENTS IN THE NEW MIDDLE AGE·GREAT MOMENTS IN THE

1967

AT&T institutes the toll-free 800 number, paving the way for the mail-order catalog boom for boomers.

1975

Miller Lite beer, the first nation- ally marketed reduced-calorie beer, hits the stands, (ful)filling our generation's vain hope that beer bellies are a thing of the past.

1983

Metropolitan Life revises "ideal weight" tables. A s man can now weigh thirt more pounds without fee a short woman, ten poun

___storage units
___hotels at Disney World
___vitamins
___lighting fixtures
___gum disease
___Harvey Keitel, naked
___the information super-
    highway
___AAA auto club
___phone sex
___sod
___Orville Redenbacher
___children's soccer leagues
___lipstick
___sports injuries
___contractors
___stocks and bonds
___Connie Chung and
    Maury Povitch
___in-laws

___pornography
___window treatments
___the weather
___sofas
___frequent-flier mileage
___roofing repairs
___seatbelts
___existence of an afterlife
___Halloween safety
___fluoride
___vibrators
___cosmetic surgery
___antidepressants
___flowering bulbs
___lawyers
___wills
___wallpaper
___no-smoking sections
___back problems
___adultery

984

first of the minivans, Dodge
[C]avan and Plymouth Voyager,
[t]he market. Ten years later,
[mo]re than 40 percent of vehi-
[cles] sold to thirty-five- to forty-
[five]-year-olds will be in this
[cat]egory.

1985

JULY 1——*Nick at Nite* debuts on
Nickelodeon. Now aging baby
boomers can relive their child-
hoods nightly while pretending
to be hip and ironic.

1987

Nabisco Brands introduces
miniature versions of childhood
favorites——Mini Oreos, Ritz Bits,
and Mini Chip-Ahoys. Originally
aimed at children, they find
their real market with weight-
conscious boomers.

____life insurance
____NPR programs
____Woody Allen's love life
____central air-conditioning
____coupons
____pantyhose brands
____taxes
____caffeine
____C-sections

____station wagons
____mortgage rates
____menopause
____ground covers
____your childhood
____tipping
____Bill Moyers
____bottled spring water
____zoning ordinances

Scoring: 10 points for each item checked off.
SCORE SO FAR _____

2. Number of years since you've

____hitchhiked
____threatened suicide over a failed love affair
____gone out dancing at midnight

DDLE AGE·GREAT MOMENTS IN THE NEW MIDDLE AGE·GREAT MOMENTS IN THE NEW

1988

AUGUST——Minoxidil, an antihypertensive drug discovered by Upjohn in the sixties, is approved by the FDA for topical use to treat hair loss. Rechristened Rogaine, it becomes the liquid promise of youth for balding boomers.

1990

Mazda introduces the moderately priced Miata, making it possible for working-class New Middle Age guys to get the hot little car of their dreams.

1991

Lands' End, Wisconsin direct mail merchants of elastic wa band jeans, comfy pajamas, and not-too-daring stirrup pants, announces that it is "readjusting its sizes," maki women's garments roomier.

___slept in your clothes

___seen all the movies nominated for the Oscar

___wanted to follow a rock band on tour

___called in sick to work because you have a hangover

___stayed in one motel room with more than three other people

___awakened and not known where you were

___crashed someone's party

___gone to the movies on a weekday afternoon

___had a new sexual partner

___smoked pot

___stayed up all night

___quit a job on impulse

___been arrested

___declared your love for someone completely inappropriate

___read *MAD* magazine

Scoring: Add up total number and multiply by 5.

Score so far _____

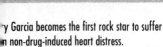

992

y Garcia becomes the first rock star to suffer
n non-drug-induced heart distress.

alie Cole wins a Grammy for performing a duet with her dead dad, Nat "King" Cole. The ultimate New Middle Age
asy: making a fortune by dominating a parent electronically.

25—Baby boomer Jay Leno replaces Johnny Carson as host of the *Tonight* show.

EMBER—Elvis-loving, pot-sniffing, female-dominated Bill Clinton is elected president of the United States.

EMBER 7—*Newsweek* features an incisive cover story on how cool it is to turn fifty.

EMBER 15—Forty-four-year-old Prince Charles becomes the first member of the royal family to go on record as
ing to become a tampon.

3. Number of friends (including yourself, if you are a lucky stiff) who have second houses _____.

Number who let you use them for free_____.

Scoring: Multiply both numbers by 20.
SCORE SO FAR _____

4. Have you ever had a sexual dream about Bill or Hillary Clinton?
___ Yes ___ No

Scoring: Give yourself 100 points for a positive answer.
SCORE SO FAR _____

1993

Mick Jagger turns fifty.

NOVEMBER 21—French performance artist Orlan, age forty-six, undergoes seventh operation on her face. The operation, performed in a Manhattan plastic surgeon's office, is transmitted via satellite for large-screen viewing in a gallery in SoHo. "I am a feminist," the artist tells *The New York Times*, "and I want to use plastic surgery to perpetuate my ideas."

5. Have you ever had a sexual dream about Dan or Marilyn Quayle?

___ Yes ___ No

Scoring: Subtract 100 points for a positive answer.

SCORE SO FAR _____

6. The Essay Section

A. *Would you read an essay on one of the following?*

___impotence
___Garry Trudeau's inner child
___choosing the right periodontist
___Bob Denver
___low-cholesterol take-out food
___Bill Clinton's thighs
___Bill Clinton's hair

1 9 9 4

RCH—Barbie turns thirty-five and still wears the same size as she did in high school.

Bean announces a gift registry for brides and grooms. A spokeswoman describes the registry as perfect for people ing married the second time with children in tow.

IL—The "Wonderbra," a push-up marvel of lingerie engineering, arrives in the United States from England. It sells in a matter of hours, thanks to glowing advance reviews by aging boomer lifestyle journalists who had journeyed ngland in pursuit of younger-looking cleavage.

IL 22—Former President Richard Milhous Nixon dies, leaving baby boomers vaguely unsatisfied: Sure, we hated him, he's lived so long, doesn't he seem more like a father figure we rebelled against and were just getting ready to forgive?

18—After undergoing artificial insemination with her husband's sperm and a donor egg, sixty-two-year-old Rosanna a Corte gives birth to a son in Rome, Italy. Her obstetrician, Dr. Severino Antinori, offers hope to all boomers still wrestling the big decision: "To want to have a child is a personal choice, and to be able to have it at any age is now possible.

___the babysitter shortage

___the man shortage

___the Beatles shortage

___airbags

___designer garbage bags

___falling in love with your personal trainer

___Rula Lenska

___time management

___Warren Beatty's commitment to fatherhood

___Warren Beatty's prostate

___Warren Beatty's former lives

___liposuction

___Bozo the Clown

___Jerry Garcia

___blue corn chips

___finding the right swimsuit

___taking your kid to school

___taking your kid to the pediatrician

___taking your kid to court

___Prozac use among character actors in Disney World

Scoring: 20 points for each essay topic.
SCORE SO FAR _____

B. *Please write a twenty-five-word essay on the above topic of your choice and sign it.*

Scoring: Subtract 100 points from your score if you were actually going to sign anything without checking the fine print first.
SCORE SO FAR _____

7. Vocabulary Quiz

Define the following:

Fruition

___A sudden feeling that you are about to be served fruit salad

___Meditation-based fertility technique

___Moisturizer that promises to restore apples to your cheeks

Sandwich Generation

___Group of people born shortly after the Pepsi Generation

___Cloning experiment gone a-rye

___Baby boomers forced to spend all disposable income on disposable diapers for their kids *and* their parents

Retin-A

___Youngest of Frank Zappa's children

___One of the good cholesterol lipids

___Miracle drug that conquers zits and wrinkles at the same time

ERT

___A quick move to avoid offensive rap music (Emergency Radio Turndown)

___One of the lovable robots on *Star Trek: Deep Space Nine*

___A little patch that can keep you buying tampons well into your sixties (Estrogen Replacement Therapy)

Downsizing

___An insidious plot by clothing manufacturers to make your clothes snugger

___Title of Lorena Bobbitt's forthcoming autobiography

___Polite term for firing people over the age of forty

Cocooning

___Television spin-off of Ron Howard's movie

___Very expensive facial treatment involving silk worms

___Tendency to become a couch caterpillar who stays home o
   Saturday nights

Blended Families

___Families that refuse to drink single-malt scotch

___Families with more than one surname

___The Brady Bunch from Hell

Miata

___Japanese herbal remedy for impotence

___One of the kids on *Beverly Hills 90201*

___Least expensive auto antidote to a midlife crisis

*Scoring: The correct answer for all, of course, is "C"—10 points
apiece. However, if you answered "A" or "B" for any of them, give
yourself 20 points apiece—being able to bullshit is what has gotten yo
this far.*

Score so far _____

8. Video Interpretation Skills

1. Do you sometimes worry that your entire family is in dange
because you are too cheap to buy a Volvo?   ___Yes ___N

2. Do certain long-distance telephone commercials bring tears t
your eyes?   ___Yes ___No

3. Do beer commercials make you believe that your friends will really come over to help you work on your house?
___ Yes ___ No

4. Are you attracted to the man or woman on the Taster's Choice spots?   ___ Yes ___ No

5. Have you ever had a serious discussion with one of your neighbors about toilet tissue, cooking oil, batteries, or douche?
___ Yes ___ No

6. Would you allow a close-up of your butt to be featured in a Docker's ad?   ___ Yes ___ No

7. If you were kidnapped by space aliens and forced to sing as many television and radio jingles for commercial products as you could remember from the last forty years to save the human race, how many would you be able to sing?   _____

Scoring: Questions 1–4: 15 points for each positive answer, 10 points for each negative response. Questions 5 and 6: 20 points for "no," 0 points for "yes." Question 7: 20 points for each jingle remembered, even if in parody version (As in "Comet, you make me vomit . . .").
TOTAL SCORE _____

WHAT THE SCORING MEANS:
1,500–2,240: High achiever, will get into all the best Automatic Teller Machines
950–1,499: Mellow, healthy, midlevel type who doesn't watch enough television
below 950: In heavy denial

Everything
I Needed to Know,
I Learned at My Twentieth
High School Reunion

Other people your age
always look older than you do.

Never tell anyone
how your life is really going.

If I didn't like someone two decades ago,
chances are he's still a jerk.

Control-top pantyhose
can only help so much.

The people who thought high school
was the best years of their lives
were probably right.

If I had married my high school sweetheart, I
would be taking Prozac now.

Stupid people do sometimes get ahead.

As life proceeds, the plot thickens—
but so do eyelashes,
chins, waistlines, and even noses.

Hair means a lot.

PART TWO

The Body Politic: Health, Fitness, and Sex

Your Health Concerns

Q *If I still have zits, why am I getting wrinkles?*

A Your anxiety about getting wrinkles is causing you to break out. The problem is not unusual—in fact, the phenomenon you describe has emerged as an important factor in the epidermally based American economy. Because we're the first generation to have exposed so much skin over a lifetime, the makers of lotions and potions have latched onto our pores and are never giving up. So you can expect to need Clearasil until you are eighty while also using the latest $35-an-ounce exfoliator and SPF 49 sun lotion.

Q *What is my prostate, and why is it always being compared to the size of fruits and nuts?*

A The prostate is a very strange organ that sometimes displays a mysterious growth spurt during a man's middle years. This could be nature's way of forcing older men to get exercise: the prostate presses on the bladder, causing them to get up and walk to the bathroom several times during televised football games. As for the fruit and nut size comparisons—in this case, bigger is not better, and you don't want to hear about anything larger than a walnut.

Q *How much cholesterol did the white paste I ate in elementar school contain?*

A Good question. An exact nutritional analysis of that tast purée is difficult to obtain because the horses used to make it ha access to more open pasture than those of today. But estimates ar not good: one dab of paste might have contained the same cho lesterol as five sticks of butter. The best you can hope is that you family ate enough of that margarine that made people sprou crowns on their heads to offset the effects. Otherwise, you migh as well give up now—your arteries started hardening even befor you knew all the words to the Pledge of Allegiance.

Q *I've just noticed that the spots on the back of my hand ar forming the constellation of my astrological sign, Aquarius. Wha does this mean?*

A You need glasses.

You and Your Changing Body

C hange is healthy. Change is a miraculous process, your body's ally. Without it, where would you be? Still wearing diapers? Still unable to balance on a two-wheeler?

Your body is changing. Is it for better or worse? Hey, let's not be judgmental here. Isn't this what personal growth is all about? Physically, midlife is a lot like adolescence: you find yourself at the mercy of hormones once again as they take leave of your system. You feel awkward. You notice that unless you exercise you have trouble fitting into your clothes. You notice that *concealing* starts to become an attractive adjective for clothes and makeup. Other forces begin to work on you, too . . .

THE FORCES OF NATURE: MEET THE BOD SQUAD

Some night soon, go out and gaze at the sky. Look up at the moon and the stars and the whole Milky Way, and say to yourself: *I am one with the universe!*

It's true. Ever since the Big Bang, matter has been scattering and compressing. Stars have been falling, and this explains why your thighs might be falling, too. As you age, the cosmic forces of nature begin to work their magic on you. Let's get to know them better, so that you can feel more positive about their startling effects on your body.

Mr. Gravity

Who is this guy, this irresistible force? For starters, he make the moon orbit around us—if not for gravity, Van Morrison' "Moondance" would not be played 146 times per day on oldie stations across the country.

Mr. Gravity also keeps you and your things down to earth Without him, you never would have been able to play Monopoly. He makes some of your favorite sexual positions feasible.

So it doesn't make any sense to blame Mr. Gravity for wanting more of you as the years go by. He's an intense guy—hi relationship with you has always had strings attached, and now he's tugging on them rather fiercely. But Mr. Gravity truly love you for yourself. He wants you to let yourself go and enjoy those relaxed-fit jeans.

Mr. Sun

What can you say about a middle-aged white dwarf star who singlehandedly made Annette Funicello beach movies and sun dried tomatoes important fixtures in American culture?

For years, we thought of the sun, a swirling mass of hydrogen gases, as our major friend, a warm guy who could always make us look better. Once upon a time people also thought it was good idea to apply blood-sucking leeches to their extremities.

Now we know better. Dermatologists tell us that the damag ing ultraviolet rays of the sun prematurely age skin, producing wrinkles and furrows. Proof? Members of the California Raisin singing group are only in their teens but look at least forty.

Body Checklist: Vital Signs That You're Definitely Mature

✓ You tweeze in places you'd never thought about before.

✓ Sucking in your gut starts to feel natural.

✓ Your eyes require special equipment for close-ups.

✓ "Flaky" describes croissants *and* your skin.

✓ You have joined the Satchel Paige school of buttocks management ("Don't look back, something might be gaining on you").

✓ You notice that dim lighting makes you look at least three years younger.

✓ Babies like to pull the flesh under your chin.

✓ You'd rather wear the same bathing suit for another summer than face the fitting-room mirror.

✓ You no longer notice each new wrinkle.

✓ When you play sports, you care less about winning than about finishing the game without getting hurt.

CLAIROL GOES CRIMINAL

Last summer I got arrested for trying to drive my car on the boardwalk in Ocean City, New Jersey. I was trying to drop off a friend of mine who can't walk well. Anyway, these cops who looked all of sixteen surrounded our car, took out their pistols à la Miami Vice, and ordered me to get out of the vehicle. It was probably the most exciting thing that had happened to them all week, arresting a forty-three-year-old woman with a cripple in her car. Filling out the arrest report, one of them asked me my hair color.

"Gray!" I barked back. He was completely bewildered. "Hey," he said, turning to his partner, "her hair is black, isn't it?" This was almost too much: not only did they look too young to be driving themselves but they were stupid as well. After a few moments I couldn't stand waiting for them to figure it out: "Ever hear of hair dye, assholes?"

The Physical Disadvantages
of Being Cool

We can blather on and on about all the options our generation has, but there are a few basic rights that middle-aged people used to enjoy that have been ripped from us:

- The right to a three-martini lunch without regret or judgment
- The right to wear funny little clear rain hats and clunky rubbers on soggy days
- The right to LET YOURSELF GO.

Two words about letting yourself go: Orson Welles. You see, it used to be quite acceptable, at a certain age, to just stop caring about what you looked like and descend into a new bodily phase. Not so nowadays. We are supposed to be keeping our thighs firm and our waists slender forever. We are supposed to exercise and tweeze and correct and camouflage so that we will always look like ever-so-slightly older versions of ourselves. We will never know the joys of not sucking in our guts. Of eating half a stick of butter without feeling like we've committed a heinous crime. Of saying, like Norman Mailer, "Oh, hell, I'm just a damned fat old man."

Remember Alfred Hitchcock? Don't expect to see Steven Spielberg deciding to make his belly a trademark. And it's doubtful that Glenn Close, Susan Sarandon, or Meryl Streep will ever go the Shelley Winters route as they age.

Are we merely vain, or extraordinarily stupid? Is all this emphasis on perpetual tautness just a plot perpetrated by Jane Fonda to pave the way for the Complete Wheelchair Fitness workout she'll be marketing in 2030?

A New Body Vocabulary

One score and a couple of years ago, some unknown wit came up with the phrase "love handles" to describe those little protrusions of fat around a beloved's waist. Love handles—*yuk!* Who would be caught dead ever using this phrase? We need hipper ways to describe the miraculous changes our bodies are undergoing. We need, in short, creative new euphemisms:

Don't Think of It As . . .	Think of It As . . .
cellulite	textural enhancement
wrinkles	relaxed-fit skin
stretch marks	epidermal highlighting
pot belly	lap shield
saddle bags	lipid storage centers
double chin	profile enhancement

BUTTERFLIES
ARE FREE

My eighteen-year-old daughter came home from college with a tattoo of an electric blender and a daisy on her shoulder.

"How could you?" I asked, referring to her lapse of taste in choosing the image.

"Oh, Mom," she groaned, "you'll never understand."

"Oh, yeah?" I said, turning around and pulling down the elastic waist on my Indian print skirt to reveal the tattoo of a butterfly on my butt. There was a stunned silence as my kid realized that tattooing technology existed before 1992.

Future Boomer
Health Problems

Every generation has a health price to pay for its behav-
ioral idiosyncracies. For our parents, the country club le‹
to tennis elbow, repetitive manual labor to carpal tunne
syndrome. But our lives have been very different, ver‹
special. Below, some boomer health problems you migh‹
see cropping up on Oprah any day now:

Air Guitar Syndrome (AGS)

Victims display unusual twisting of hips and fluttering of
fingers that can strike during business meetings or even
during meals. Sometimes the frantic motions are accom-
panied by blustering verbal tics. The only known cure:
eight hours of polka music daily for six months.

Cheap Charter Syndrome (CCS)

Sitting in a theater, on a bus, or even in a car, sufferers
will begin to develop leg cramps and severe neurologica‹
glitches, blabbering on in pidgin Dutch about their trip to
Europe in the summer of 1971.

Earth–Shoe Tendon Syndrome (ESTS)

Years of being strangely shod in shoes that dipped backward at the heel finally takes its toll on ESTS patients, whose tendons became relaxed beyond what can be accommodated in normal footwear. ESTS might take years to show up, but when it does, therapy consists of wearing triangular, backward-sloping foam wedges affixed to the outside of one's shoes. (Clever sufferers can disguise these as a new kind of "platform" heel.)

Hitchhiker's Thumb Syndrome (HTS)

Normally, the human thumb is opposable, but those afflicted with this syndrome often weren't opposed to going anywhere with anyone for months on end. In HTS, the thumb frequently returns to that extended position, and sufferers are forced to become politicians who favor the thumbs-up sign or children's folksingers who can disguise the syndrome by strumming a guitar.

Split Ends Syndrome (SES)

Almost exclusively female, this syndrome strikes middle-aged boomers of all hair lengths. The symptoms: excessive tossing of head, neurotic kneading of thumbs while humming old commercials for Herbal Essence shampoo.

Waterbed Vertigo Syndrome (WVS)

Usually occurs during orgasm, when sufferer will begin to feel dizzy, imagine hearing rain, and wonder if he or she has rolled up the windows on the VW bug.

One Pill
Makes You Smaller . . .
Products We'd Like to See in
the Drugstore

Movie Star Band-Aids
Forget Mickey and the Ninja Turtles. We want Liam Neeson or Sharon Stone wrapped around our little fingers.

Home Menopause Kit
Pee into a cup: if there is a long pause before it turns blue, you'll finally know that latest surge of warmth wasn't due to the spicy bean dip.

Medical Cleavage Tape
For that no-bra look: healthy support that lets the skin breathe.

"Gee, Your Hair Came Back, That's Terrific" Shampoo
This would be infinitely more popular than its predecessor, "Gee, Your Hair Smells Terrific."

Transparent Collagen Post-Its
For those last-minute temporary touch-ups.

Embarrassed by the Light:
A Maturing Young Woman's
Guide to Makeup

Hey, girls—we grew up wanting to look natural, and now there's a price to pay, since we still want to look natural but better.

Skin Stuff

If you are looking for a full-time hobby or have a spare hundred dollars you don't know what to do with, try taking care of your skin in the multistep system recommended by saleswomen in department stores.

1. Use a deep cleanser. It is always labeled "deep," but one wonders if it's not really shallow, because afterward your skin is left vaguely unsatisfied and confused, so you have to use . . .

2. A clarifier. This is to help clear up any ideas your pores might have that they can just hang out unopened on your face. Next, it's good to use . . .

3. An exfoliator. (*Exfoliator!* starring Brigitte Nielsen . . . She came, she saw, she *sloughed!*) You have to get the dead skin cells off your puss, to get it ready for . . .

4. The five-minute deep-cleansing mask. A little like putting Play-Doh on your face, but a lot more expensive. And, finally . . .

5. The moisturizer, which has a name that either sounds like a minor character in a Marquis de Sade novel *or* a race horse. (Rénergie . . . Smart Move . . .) All the verbs describing these moisturizers have *hydro* in them, and you are encouraged to think of your epidermis drinking at the trough of eternal youth.

Eyes

We don't want to use those terms *bags* and *wrinkles*, but the cosmetic companies aren't so shy. Their products promise to tighten up eye areas and make under-eye shadows nearly invisible. The advertisements show models like Isabella Rossellini, who made a pact with Satan back in 1978: "Let me star in really bad Hollywood movies without ever aging, and I'll give you my mom Ingrid Bergman's recipe for Swedish meatballs."

Lips

Did you know that a woman's natural lip line begins disintegrating after age thirty-five, and she has to use a lipliner or she will be mistaken for an old hag? No? Neither did I until I made the expensive mistake of going to the department store makeup counter

---

A NEW BODY OF CLASSICS

There is a desperate need for good information on health topics. The following large-print guides, based on children's literature, could come in handy.

Pat the Fat: A Touch-and-Feel Book   Explore and celebrate the tactile diversity of stored lipids without bothering yourself or anyone else. Includes cuddly pages of cellulite, double chins, and belly blubber.

The Itsy-Bitsy Spider (Vein)   A delightful look at outpatient laser surgery. An excerpt: "The itsy-bitsy spider vein went up the leg so stout/In came the doc and ripped the spider out..."

See (Liver) Spot   Follow the antics of those pesky age freckles as they cavort across the page: "See (Liver) Spot. See (Liver) Spot grow..."

The Sexual Evolution

Is there a New Middle Age sex scene?
Perhaps it's more of a predicament than a scene.

In a nutshell:
You're either married with no time to have sex,
or single with no time to find someone
to have sex with. For married couples with
young children, the best foreplay consists of
getting a babysitter.

You can also turn to the time-honored
middle-age strategy of repression.
We have a much better array of gadgets and
techniques than were available to our parents.

Sex substitutes for males:
leaf blowers, chain saws, frequent-flier mileage,
Harleys, remote controls, Powerbooks

Sex substitutes for women:
shoe buying, leg waxing, aerobics, Thighmasters,
juicers, spa getaways, Fabio

Twin Peaks? We Wish

Women hit their sexual peak some time between the ages o
thirty-five and forty-five. Guys reach theirs at about nineteen
You do the calculations.

So for now we'll leave the guys out of it. Because they are
(And it's only fair, since we have PMS and menopause to cop
with.)

Women—how do you know when you are at the absolut
summit of your sexuality? Take this little quiz.

ARE
YOU ON TOP?
THE SEX PEAK QUIZ

1. **When I see a cute guy in his twenties, I want to**
   a. get a body transplant and ask him on a date
   b. impress him with stories of how I saw The Monkees liv
   in concert once
   c. kidnap him and take him to a hotel that has Trojans an
   K-Y jelly on the room service menu
2. **When a guy takes his shirt off on television, I**
   a. faint
   b. begin counting his chest hairs
   c. start rolling the videotape to record the moment for m
   "Hope Chest" collection of half-naked torsos
3. **I can have more than one orgasm**
   a. with a really special lover
   b. with a really special battery-operated friend
   c. standing in line at the supermarket

Scoring: Three "C" answers mean that you are at the peak RIGHT NOW! What are you doing wasting time reading books? Two "C" answers: you're six months away. One "C" answer: you have entered the extended foreplay, prepeak time, which can last up to two years. No "C" answers? Let's hope you're a late bloomer.

Make Love and War: Sex and Dating

Q *I'm a single guy, thirty-nine, and my life is miserable. Once in a while I find a woman who wasn't screwed over by her ex-husband, or one who actually has a paying job or who was alive when Sonny and Cher were still together, and we go out. But the rest of the time I hang out with my married friends, and that's my social life. I'm a sidecar on the motorcycle of someone else's marriage. What should I do?*

A Be sure to wear a helmet.

Q *I have been dating for nearly thirty years with no discernibl[e] results. Friends of mine have been married, had kids, gotten di[vorced], and changed their sexual orientation, all while I'm stil[l] hanging around laundromats trying to meet guys. Is this normal[?]*

A Absolutely. Men don't do their laundry very often, an[d] women have been known to need as long as fifty years to mee[t] an eligible bachelor in a wash-and-dry setting. You could kee[p] trying, but face it—by forty, many guys actually own washin[g] machines they don't use, either. Appliance-oriented dating is dif[ficult] as you age—I suggest you get a dog. Men who own dog[s] actually have to walk them, at least if they live alone.

Q *I love my wife. I still find her exciting, and we have a goo[d] sex life. Here's my problem, though: every once in a while she goe[s] haywire and tries to enliven our sexual sessions by dressing up i[n] Victoria's Secret garter belts and teddies and other stuff. She get[s] mad at me because I start laughing when I see her in thos[e] "erotic" outfits. Cavorting around with some tart in split-crotc[h] red-lace panties reminds me of something some old middle-age[d] guy would do, not me. Shouldn't she be flattered that I'm turne[d] on by the sight of her in old cotton underwear?*

A Rarely have I heard from such an insensitive asshole. You'r[e] letting your fear of lingerie ruin a beautiful shopping experienc[e] for your wife. You should be flattered. She could have bough[t] shoes. She could have bought a bread-baking machine, or a lap[-]top computer, or all sorts of other merchandise that would no[t] contribute one iota to your sexual pleasure. So stop complaining[.] If you have to, close your eyes and dream of white cotton jock[-]ies, you ex-hippie pervert, you.

Checklist: Signs That You Have Reached Sexual Maturity

✓ You become curious about etiquette tips for attending a friend's third or fourth wedding.

✓ While walking down the street, you have the strange sensation of having become invisible to the opposite sex.

✓ In bed, you are grateful to have become a bit nearsighted.

✓ You no longer make love to "Knights in White Satin" or "In a Gadda da Vida."

✓ You are beginning to realize that the Battle of the Sexes is not really a war but a series of skirmishes in which many hostages are taken.

✓ While having sex, you begin to fantasize about yourself—younger, thinner, hairier, etc.

✓ Except on rare occasions, you are much less likely to make a fool of yourself for sex.

✓ You would like to go to bars to find exciting sexual partners, but you can't stay up late enough.

✓ Phone sex doesn't appeal to you because you spend too much time on the phone at work.

✓ You can actually be at the same party with one or more ex-lovers without totally freaking out.

I'm a Believer—Our Generation's Love Affair with Serial Monogamy

It's ridiculously ironic that the folks who ushered in the sexua[l] revolution would end up getting married so frequently. But w[e] do, and it's going to cause a lot of confusion at cemeteries year[s] from now. Serial monogamy has become, for many of us, the per[-] formance art of love. I am a serial monogamist myself (Two down[,] more to go?) and proud of it, but every once in a while I get [a] creepy feeling that maybe there is more in common between se[-] rial murder and serial monogamy than I would like to admit.

Serial Monogamy and Serial Homicide, Some Connections?

Serial Monogamy	Serial Homicide
Victims of shallow relationships	Victims in shallow graves
In beginning: "He's such a nice man— he could never hurt me."	Neighbors: "He is such a nice, quiet man—I can't imagine him hurting anyone."
Feel compulsion to mate	Feel compulsion to kill

Serial Divorce

Feel compulsion to kill mate

Stuck in the Middle with U: Catalog of Continuing Education Courses

---

POP CULTURE REIDENTIFICATION

Learn how television and movies influenced your sense of self, and develop new strategies for coming to grips with getting older. Which characters did you identify with when you were younger, and how can you shift that allegiance now? Issues include: *Womanhood:* Moving from Goldie Hawn to Ruth Buzzie and then back to Goldie. *Manhood:* The Beverly Hillbillies, from Jethro to Jed. *Intellectual development:* Shifting from Gilligan to the Professor. *Superheroes:* Was Adam West's relationship with Julie Newmar on the old *Batman* series healthy? Is Michael Keaton the ultimate middle-aged Batman: slightly balding, and willing to leave Kim Basinger behind when his beeper sounds?

TIME: MWF 9 P.M. EASTERN STANDARD TIME/ 8 P.M. CENTRAL & PACIFIC

FINDING YOUR INNER TEENAGER

He or she is in there, hanging out. . . that carefree self who still goes out on weeknights and can drink that extra bottle of wine without ill effects. Using as its text Dr. Cornelia Spry's *When Life Was Fun: Satuated Fats, Alcohol, Drugs, and Unsafe Sex,* this meditative course will get you back in touch with the immature, irresponsible you. Participants are asked to prepare by skipping work for no reason at all at least once before the class begins. Please bring your own lava lamp and rolling papers—other materials will be provided.

TIME: LUNAR AND SOLAR ECLIPSE DAYS, 1995–2001

GOING BACK INTO THE CLOSET:
THE STORAGE IMPERATIVE

If the seventies were about sex and the eighties about money, wha
are the nineties all about? Storage. By the time you reach the middl
of life, you have accumulated a lot of stuff. This course will teach yo
where to put it and explain how it is possible to spend more money o
closet organization than you did on your first automobile. Please brin
a copy of the Hold Everything catalog to the first class. No wire hang
ers allowed.

TIME: MONDAYS AT 7 P.M., UNTIL YOU GET IT RIGHT

MY MOTHER THE MINIVAN:
AUTOMOBILE CHANNELING

Baba Ford Dos of the Guru Garage will teach you how to use your ca
phone and New Age music tapes to get in touch with dead loved ones
Break through to the other side even while you are stuck in traffic
Warning: As of press date, we have yet to determine cellular phon
rates for cosmic conversations.

TIME: BE HERE NOW!

OVERCOMING
CALENDAR AND POST-IT DEPENDENCY

Do you go into a catatonic fit if you misplace your calendar? Are you unable to remember your spouse's name when he or she calls unless it is written on a Post-It attached to your office phone? This course was designed to reintroduce the concept of internal memory to your life. Beginning, gradual exercises will enable you to recall your agenda during a one-hour stretch without consulting calendars or notes. The eventual goal of the class is to get students to spend one calendar-free weekday without anxiety. Advanced students are encouraged to repeat the class and learn to go around without wearing a watch for one twenty-four-hour period.

TIME: **MTTH 2–4 P.M., OR TWF 3–5 P.M., OR**
 WFS 2:15–4:15 P.M., OR MWF 1–2 P.M. *AND*
 TTH 2:45–3:45 P.M.

BOTTLED WATER TASTING:
AN ARMCHAIR TOUR OF THE WORLD'S GREATEST
WATER-PRODUCING REGIONS

Climate, geology, thermal energy—all of these greatly influence the bouquet and taste of bottled water. This six-session, hands-on course will tell you everything you need to know when choosing a water in a restaurant or for your home table. Learn to read a water label, and to correctly pronounce the names of delicious calorie-free potables from France, Italy, New England, California, Arkansas, Maine, and Iceland. Spitting buckets will be provided to prevent bloating.

TIME: SEATINGS AT **6 P.M.** AND **9 P.M. MF**

Not Flossing
as a Subversive Activity,
or Living Dangerously Now

• • •

Hey, kids—we're still risk-takers.
It's just that the stakes are a bit higher (or lower,
depending on how you look at it). Whereas
hitchhiking used to give you a rush, or dropping
acid from an unknown source was a groove, now
we can go crazy in any number of new ways:

Drinking caffeinated
coffee after 8 P.M.

Ordering the minivan
without the airbags

Getting a tan

Installing unauthorized
software

Throwing away receipts or
warranty cards

Not changing the oil
filter every 3,000 miles

Buying the generic brand

Ordering dessert

Refinancing your mortgage

Drinking tap water

Not flossing

Sitting in a smoking
section

Using latex over oil paint

Canceling your automobile
club membership

Bicycling without a helmet

Not getting the three-year
extended-service contract on
appliances

Having a drink
at lunch

PART THREE

The Days of Our Lifestyles.... Food, Clothing, Shelter, and Entertainment

Life Terms

Our parents had lives. We have *lifestyles.* Lives just happen, but lifestyles are *created* by creative people in unique generations such as ours.

Conversationally, the lives of our middle-aged parents were pretty boring, but we can talk about our lifestyles endlessly because we've invented more descriptive phrases for our daily activities and concerns.

Life Vocabulary (our parents)	*Lifestyle Vocabulary (us)*
decorating	interior design
spinster	career woman
divorced mother	single parent
sloppy	casual
TV dinner	microwavable entrée
record player	sound system
beautician	stylist
troubled	dysfunctional
sunburn	UV damage
carpet and linoleum	floor coverings
full of yourself	empowered

Life Vocabulary (our parents)	*Lifestyle Vocabulary (us)*
raising kids	parenting
pills	medications
vitamins	nutritional supplements
sick	chronically ill
snacking	grazing
cold cream	exfoliator
necklaces and scarves	accessories
jobs	careers
hobbies	being "into" something
emotional problems	personal growth
boss	manager
hillbilly	country
smart	gifted
stupid	challenged
exercise	workout
getting older	aging
saving string	recycling
planting shrubs	landscaping
porches	decks
confused	open
the blues	depression

LIFESTYLE PORN:
THE CONCEPT

*W*e boomers need to be constantly excited about our lives. As we get older, it gets harder to become instantly aroused by our own possibilities, so we turn to lifestyle porn to give us the thrills we crave. Lifestyle porn can come in many forms, but it shares a particular look and attitude that we like. The people, houses, cars, and dinner parties depicted in lifestyle porn are exactly how we imagine our lives should be or will be one day.

The most pornographic film of the 1990s was *Home Alone.* Why? Because it depicts a boomer family with four children who live in a $500,000 home in a posh Chicago suburb, own every gadget you can imagine, and can afford to go to Paris for Christmas.

The ultimate porno novel of the premillennial years is *The Bridges of Madison County.* A forty-four-year-old Iowa woman who, even after having two children, is marvelously slim and taut, just happens to meet a ravishingly handsome *National Geographic* photographer who, at age fifty-six, has a stomach like a washboard and the ability to have sex more than six times a day. Her husband just happens to be away for four days, showing pigs at the county fair. The woman and the photographer make love constantly all over the house but also engage in soul-stirring conversations late into the night. The photographer leaves and the woman's husband never finds out. Later in her life, she discovers that the photographer never got over her and spent his twilight years babbling about her beauty in jazz bars and begging musicians to write songs about her. Other lifestyle porn includes:

- Upscale glossy food, decorating, and gardening magazines, especially the ones where we read about some boomer celebrity's yurt mountaintop retreat furnished with Gustav Stickley furniture and attached to the geodesic greenhouse where she grows mesclun salads that she serves with the warm goat cheese she makes from her own herd's milk.

- Any catalogs featuring stylish solutions to the chaos of our lives: J. Peterman (mail-order Hemingway), Williams-Sonoma, Levenger, Hold Everything!, The Sharper Image, Hammacher Schlemmer, Smith & Hawken, Gardener's Eden, etc.

- Ice cream flavors that shamefully celebrate bizarre food tastes that we formerly kept private, like chocolate chip cookie dough mushed into ice cream.

- Car commercials convincing us that family sedans are actually as sexy as sportscars.

- Movies or TV shows in which working couples effortlessly juggle careers and home without full-time domestic help and somehow also find the time to perfectly coordinate their wardrobes and get their hair styled daily.

- First-person essays suggesting that every mundane event, from doing laundry to picking up a kid at school to picking out one's first bifocals, are moments suitable for intense emotional epiphanies.

How to Know If
You Are Reading a BoomerMag

• • •

1. **The cover features**
    a. some forty-five-year-old movie star who, either through a pact with the devil, cosmetic surgery, or heavy airbrushing, looks more vibrant than you did at the age of twelve
    b. a gripping lifestyle topic such as buying a house, improving your marital sex life, or building a better deck
    c. a provocative question the likes of which you might want to explore after about three beers: When Is Work Too Much? Is Adultery Worth It? Why Does America Love Howard Stern?

2. **The columnists tackle**
    a. your finances
    b. your children's behavior
    c. your health
    d. your real estate investments

3. **The recipes contain**
    a. low fat content
    b. strategies for throwing a six-course dinner party with only an hour-and-a-half preparation
    c. tips for adapting Mongolian cuisine to the microwave

Is There a Doctor in the Kitchen?

April 1994. First boomers Bill and Hillary Clinton become the first presidential couple to hire a physician to design low-fat meals in conjunction with the White House chef. Dr. Dean Ornish, a diet guru, tries to wean Bill Clinton away from Big Macs and on to soyburgers.

Menu Specials

Since our generation invented sex, we can't rely on it to make u guilty. But aging requires *some* sense of morality, and in searching fo a new moral scapegoat we have found the perfect substitute: *food*

It's the new double standard: we take the wholesome food home to meet the family, all the time longing for the "dirty" fas foods that really excite us. We want grease. We want salt. We want sugar. But we feel terribly guilty every time we scarf down that pint of Ben and Jerry's Heathbar Crunch. We hate ourselves the next morning.

Being DC—Dietarily Correct—is a strain. Friends call friends and confess their strange longings and the gustatory sins they have committed recently. The worst moment is when we're out with friends for lunch or dinner and the waiter asks: "Can I interest anyone in dessert?"

There is a dead silence and then some nervous giggling. The waiter might have asked if anyone was interested in going hunting for spotted owls, or marketing a personal lubricant made out of orca whale blubber.

Everyone looks down at the table. It is the moment of reckoning, and one of two things will happen. Either we will all feel too guilty to say "yes," and there will be a brisk compensatory round of ordering decaffeinated beverages. Or one brave soul, looking for another lemming tart to jump off the cliff with him, will ask if anyone else plans to indulge. Perhaps several others will avow that they could manage to *share* one or two pieces of a succulent last course. The waiter will leave and return with several sinful platefuls and thousands of forks. While he is gone, the table will be buzzing with titillating talk of how bad we are being. Once the desserts arrive and consumption begins, everyone will moan and smack their lips in ways that seldom used to be seen outside the bedroom and basically ask each other over and over, "Was it good for you?"

Come on Baby, Light My Gas Barbecue... Food and Entertainment

Q *A long time ago I thought I saw a recipe for Evian sorbet on a Martha Stewball program on PBS. Could you find it for me?*

A We called Ms. Stewball and she agreed to supply the recipe for this light, refreshing dessert.

Evian Sorbet
(serves 20)

Ingredients: one quart Evian water, preferably from glass rather than plastic bottle ("The difference in taste is remarkable," says Ms. Stewball).

Step 1: Scour your local antique store for metal candy molds in the shape of perennial flowers, benign insects, or endangered reptiles.

Step 2: Locate a restaurant supplier that can rent or sell you a freezer unit capable of freezing quiescent concoctions. Have it delivered to your house, but remember to call the electrician first to put in a special line that will be able to handle it.

Step 3: Pour Evian into molds and freeze overnight. Spray rose-colored handblown sherbet glasses lightly with Evian mister and unmold sorbet into them. Serve immediately.

(Nutritional analysis: Calories: 0. Fat: 0 grams. Cholesterol: 0 grams. Sugar: 0 grams. Moral superiority: 100 percent)

Note: "You could make this in ordinary ice cube trays in your kitchen freezer," says Ms. Stewball, "but the presentation impact won't be nearly the same, and the taste much less rich."

Q *Why don't I give as many parties as I used to? It really bothers me.*

A Did you read that first question? Your fear of entertaining might well stem from the Martha Stewball Factor. I mean, not all of us have the time to decorate our horse barn with sprays of freesias or carve pumpkins to look like Victorian gargoyles, for chrissakes!

But let's look at other current party inhibitors. In your twenties, what constituted a party? Six-packs and potato chips. You didn't clean the place because you knew it would be trashed anyway. Sometimes you even moved out of a place after giving a party.

No wonder we don't give as many parties. The party stakes are higher now, and the etiquette is trickier. First, no one eats that many potato chips anymore. Probably because they never arrive already stoned. Come to think of it, no one drinks that much beer anymore, either. So parties are someplace you go to stand around and talk. When you're sober, you notice how clean or dirty someone's place is. When you don't eat five pounds of Doritos in a single evening, you expect more from the cuisine.

There's very little sexual suspense, too. When was the last time you went to a party and someone went home with someone else unexpectedly?

Geez, I'm depressed. Want to come over and have a drink?

New, Lite Programming on the Food Channel

6 A.M. COOKING WITH BODY HEAT The aerobics routine that lets you get fit while preparing low-fat meals for your entire family in specially sealed bags under your arms and between your thighs. (Anyone can participate, but for best results, purchase your special William Hurt Body Heat bodywear at the K-Mart nearest you.)

9 A.M. HONEY, THEY SHRUNK THE FOOD! Join boomers Brad and Susan as they explore exciting new miniature varieties of old favorites—mini-pecan-sandies, mini-piz-zas, mini-hamburgers, mini-hoagies, mini-leg-of-lamb, mini-pretzels, mini-hog's feet, mini-pies . . . *Today:* Is a cornish game hen merely a mini-chicken, and can you feed a family of four with it?

10 A.M. LEAN CUISINE CRAFTS Host Kathy Lee shows you fabulous things to do with those little plastic trays from frozen diet entrées. *Today:* Make your own computer diskettes!

3 P.M. and 11:30 P.M. daily. MILK AND COOKIES A virtual-reality snacking experience—watch small children consume fatty, butter-filled cookies and *whole* milk! Soothing, satisfying, and calorie-free. (Pick up our scratch-and-sniff cards at your local supermarket for the complete experience, plus the new product from Liquid Paper, "Milk Moustache," and you'll swear it's your snack, too.)

8 P.M. THE MAN WHO MISTOOK HIS WIFE FOR A STICK OF BUTTER Hosts Oliver Sacks and Wolfgang Puck interview patients at mental institutions across the country, encouraging them to talk about their culinary hallucinations. *Today:* schizophrenics who love Doublemint chewing gum.

IT'S MY PARTY
AND I'LL CRY IF
I WANT TO

My poor wife. She meant well. For my fortieth birthday, she booked a restaurant and invited all my friends and colleagues to a surprise party. Then one of the idiots I work with convinced her that having a stripper there would be really funny. Yeah. Having a naked woman sit on my lap and thrust her breasts toward my mouth while everyone I know, including my mother and my twelve-year-old son, watched me, was <u>hilarious</u>. So funny I forgot to laugh. For my fiftieth, I'm going to a Tibetan monastery.

CineMid:
Comfy Little Movies
We Love

We've always been wild for movies, and now some of us are even making them, which you can tell because 40 percent of the latest releases are simply bloated versions of the TV shows we used to watch. (What would the world be like if Ingmar Bergman had been influenced by *The Flintstones* or *Sargeant Bilko*?)

Since people our age started making blockbuster movies, near stuff can happen. The parents in kiddie flicks can smoke dope or get divorced or experience gender confusion. Guys over forty can have passionate romances with their psychiatrists. A lawyer can turn out to be Peter Pan and fly off to fight pirates on a new kind of active Club Med vacation.

Renting these movies only reinforces what we all know: we're still cool kids with feature-length possibilities.

• • •

SOME HOT CINEMID VIDEOS,
AND WHY WE LOVE THEM

Dave: My husband has disappeared, and in his place there's a guy who looks exactly like him, but he's funnier, sexier, and more sensitive.

City Slickers: If only I could take time off to learn how to rope and deliver calves, I'd get that promotion.

Parenthood: Gee, if even Steve Martin and Rick Moranis find parenting stressful, I guess I'm doing okay.

Basic Instinct: Where on earth did she get that icepick? I can never find cool stuff like that at my hardware store.

Bull Durham: Maybe I can't compete against young studs or play ball anymore, but I could still end up with Susan Sarandon.

Fatal Attraction: My husband will never have an affair because he likes our kids' pet rabbit too much.

The Piano: I've always wanted a man who would dust my fine furniture in the nude.

• • •

ENTERTAINMENT FIGURES, THEN AND NOW

Our parents had . . .	*We have . . .*
Bob Hope	Jay Leno
Lawrence Welk	Harry Connick Jr.
Jackie Gleason	Roseanne
Liberace	Elton John
Judy Garland	Barbra Streisand
Carol Burnett	Tracey Ullman
Jack LaLanne	Susan Powter

Video Dating, Midlife Style

● ● ●

It's a hassle to go out, or sometimes you can't. Often you and your beloved decide to get a tape and hunker down on the couch. Amazing, isn't it, that you can go to a store and bring back a slab of plastic that contains *any movie in the world you'd want to see?*

Yes, the VCR was an amazing technological development. But we are still interpreting its social consequences for our generation. The idea of staying at home and enjoying a movie together always starts out fun. But in choosing that tape for your video date, you and your lover cross the biggest minefield in the eternal battle of the sexes. Yes, the video store has thousands of selections to choose from. So why can't you find one that seems appealing to both of you? Because, as you can see here, it doesn't exist:

WHAT WOMEN WANT in a video . . .	WHAT MEN WANT in a video . . .
Relationships, good kissing, good story, Daniel Day Lewis	Tit shots, explosions, guys their own age who not only stand up to their bosses but save entire airports or planets

What woman hasn't wanted to scream when her partner comes back after forty-five minutes toting a Schwarzenegger flick and *Emanuelle IX?* What guy hasn't drifted off into polite slumber at

Goldie and Kurt cavort on some yacht, or Daniel Day Lewis kisses some broad's gloves?

A savvy video producer could easily solve this problem and become rich at the same time by providing *blended movies* for the VCR date. Let's face it, who cares that much about plot when you're watching a movie together on Friday night? You're tired. You just want the highlights. And there should be someone out there who could splice together movies creatively to provide high points for one partner while the other one takes a bathroom or snack break.

The movie could start out as a Merchant/Ivory novel adaptation with some excellent period antiques and a passionately romantic scene on the canals of Venice. Suddenly, a shot would ring out . . . and CUT TO Steven Seagal chasing Chinese warlords through San Marco square. Seagal is just getting into totally mutilating them when . . . CUT TO Anjelica Huston, as a warlord's wife in New York, who is flirting with Daniel Day Lewis in a loincloth. But Daniel has just invited Jack Nicholson over to watch some television . . . CUT TO montage of last year's NCAA tournament highlights . . .

Think of movie blending as a sort of cinematic Muzak for weary lovers. Male and female would both be better couch viewers if we could only acknowledge that, like simultaneous orgasms, simultaneous movie thrills rarely occur.

You have two VCRs and want to create your own blended Friday-night film? Here are some ideas:

Babette's Feast	and	*The Microwave Massacre*
The Dead	and	*Night of the Living Dead*
Green Card	and	*Behind the Green Door*

Rolling Credits Life Quiz

● ● ●

Do you ever get the feeling that you're in a movie, that your life isn't really happening to you? A lot of us do. What's your movie— Hitchcock or Altman? Coppola or Campion? As the first intensely celluloid generation, we have a hard time separating real life from reel versions. But at least it makes our personal conversations easier since we've developed cinematic shortcuts to discuss our problems and experiences. ("What was labor like? Well, remember that scene in *Alien,* where the monster pops out of John Hurt's stomach . . .")

Use this quickie cinema quiz to determine your own life's movie rating.

1. My dating experiences remind(ed) me of
(circle as many as you like)
Annie Hall
McCabe and Mrs. Miller
Body Heat
Marat/Sade
Bonnie and Clyde
Tootsie
When Harry Met Sally
The Way We Were
9½ Weeks
My Beautiful Laundrette
Jules and Jim
Love Story
Maurice
Making Mr. Right

The Philadelphia Story
Starman
No Way to Treat a Lady
Harold and Maude
Tell Me That You Love Me, Junie Moon
Henry and June
Fritz the Cat
Casablanca
Godzilla

2. When I get together with close friends, it seems like
The Big Chill
Return of the Secaucus Seven
Alien
Stand by Me
Casablanca
Whatever Happened to Baby Jane?

My Dinner with Andre
King of Hearts
Gallipoli
Hook
Parenthood
American Graffiti
Heathers
The Green Berets
Seven Samurai
Meatballs
Peter's Friends
Much Ado About Nothing
Picnic at Hanging Rock
Woodstock
The Group
Night of the Living Dead

3. My last vacation reminded me of

National Lampoon's Vacation
Gidget Goes Hawaiian
The Sheltering Sky
Enchanted April
Apocalypse Now
Airport
North by Northwest
The Roman Spring of Mrs. Stone
Patriot Games
Planes, Trains, and Automobiles
The Out-of-Towners
Casablanca
Home Alone
Easy Rider
Blue Lagoon
The Parent Trap
Beach Blanket Bingo
The Year of Living Dangerously

4. My marriage reminds me of

The Thin Man
Kramer vs. Kramer
Casablanca
It's a Wonderful Life
Shoot the Moon

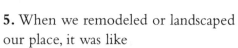

5. When we remodeled or landscaped our place, it was like

The Money Pit
It's a Wonderful Life
The Terminator
Bridge over the River Kwai

Swiss Family Robinson
The War Between the Roses
Mr. Blandings Builds His Dream House
The Wilderness Family
Casablanca
Mosquito Coast
Flight of the Phoenix
Out of Africa
The Towering Inferno
The Field

6. My boss reminds me of
Nurse Ratchet in *One Flew over the Cuckoo's Nest*
Rick in *Casablanca*
Faye Dunaway in *Network*
George Kennedy in *Cool Hand Luke*
Orson Welles in *Citizen Kane*
Captain Bligh in *Mutiny on the Bounty*
Robert Duvall in *The Great Santini*
Matthew Broderick in *Glory*
Demi Moore in *Disclosure*

7. My drug experiences were like
Altered States
Midnight Express
Pee Wee's Big Adventure
Naked Lunch
Beetlejuice
Casablanca
The Wizard of Oz

8. My relationship with my mother reminds me of

Terms of Endearment

Mrs. Doubtfire

Carrie

Mommy Dearest

Psycho

Ratings:

(X)cellent: 60 or over circled

(R)'nt You Cool: 45 or over circled

(P)retty (G)ood: 20 or over circled

(G)et a (Reel) Life: 19 or under circled

Clothing Allowances

As a generation, we invented informality. We lived in blue jeans and T-shirts. On weekends, we still do. A whole fashion industry has been dedicated to making sure that we will be able to wear blue jeans and T-shirts forever.

It was getting hard to sit down in our jeans, so they gave us relaxed fit and elastic sides. When it gets hard to stand up in our jeans, they'll give us denim lap throws with stitched pockets and studs.

The T-shirts just get bigger, more oversized with the passing years. They don't sport offensive slogans like "Shit Happens." They're more likely to be from Banana Republic than from a Grateful Dead concert.

And here's the really great news: Even when we get old, we'll never have to wear those little old lady orthopedic shoes, since essentially running shoes *are* orthopedic shoes, and we already wear them with everything, even tuxedos.

Of course, we might need ergonomically designed hiking boots for the older foot. Walking shoes are already big sellers. We'll probably be the first generation to wear specially designed sitting shoes, limping shoes, and shuffling shoes. (Instead of air in "the pump," how about hot water?)

Checklist: Clothing Signs That You Are Growing Up

✓ You actually own a pair of "dressy" blue jeans with an ironed crease down each leg.

✓ Your wardrobe is tending toward the slimming darker shades. (In fact, some people might mistake your closet for a priest's or mortician's.)

✓ You probably have the right lingerie to go under see-through blouses.

✓ Your monthly dry cleaning bill comes to more than your allowance in college was.

✓ You have stopped keeping shoes that hurt you.

✓ You're less likely to tuck everything in.

The Tropical Salad of CocoonWear

You know the type of clothing I'm talking about. It's advertised in glossy yet understated catalogs with models who are really twenty-three but they're meant to look mature because they're photographed without lipliner. They are standing in archways or sitting around on the stone wall of a deserted country mill with cute members of the opposite sex, or taking their perfect blond children kayaking in a bubbling Vermont stream.

Hey, you can identify. You crave these clothes. In these duds you can do just about anything and look cool. Sleep. Walk your dog. Watch TV. Run out to the convenience store. Go to dinner parties. Take long flights.

These clothes are all 100 percent combed, prewashed, preshrunk, lot-dyed, bias cut, third world loomed, comfy, and stretchy and don't mind a bit if you eat that extra piece of cheesecake after dinner.

The catalogs use words and phrases for these clothes that you see in personal ads—sensuous, witty, sense of fun and adventure, flexible, warm, easygoing. You're not buying sweatshirt tunics, you're buying companions that will caress you all day and night.

And the colors! They're made up of:

- Expensive tropical fruits that you think about twice before buying at the supermarket—mango, avocado, guava . . .
- Substances only found in jewelry stores or wholesale on overseas vacations—onyx, jade, garnet . . .
- Subtle, smelly, dirty things that you'd never truly think would look good on your back—moss, pebble, sand, lichen . . . (They never use colors that would perhaps appeal to more indoorsy types, like "tobacco stain," "bruise," and "jaundice.")

You can never have enough of these clothes, and you have to buy the tops and bottoms together, because how are you ever going to match anything with a tangerine fisherman's sweater or chardonnay stirrup pants?

The Closet

CLOTHING ITEMS YOU ONCE
NEVER IMAGINED YOU WOULD NEED

The Victoria's Secret "Miracle" push-up bra

French gardening clogs

"Figure-flattering" bathing suit
with "miracle net tummy reducer" panel

Any shirt with verticle stripes

Especially long tunics

Japanese gardening pants

MILLENNIAL CATALOG PORN: THE "A" LIST

Victoria's Secret

J. Peterman

Smith & Hawken

J. Crew

Clifford & Wills

Tweeds

Land's End

L.L. Bean

Hanna Andersen
(the Mommy clothes)

Garnet Hill

Clothing

Q *When I see the stuff we wore back in the late sixties and seventies coming back, it makes me feel old. Should I try to wear these clothes the second time around, or just keep gauzy Indian tunics as a wonderful memory?*

A Use your own discretion, and perhaps the opinion of an honest friend who will tell you when you look like a nincompoop. A lot of people our age were hurt back in the Great Bell Bottom Scare of 1994, when they didn't realize that it requires a certain flair to cavort in bells once again. Liza Minnelli was the principal celebrity victim.

Q *My mother says that control-top pantyhose are nothing more than disposable girdles. Is this true?*

A Even if it is, it's worth the extra $580 you will spend during a lifetime to never utter the word *girdle*.

CLOTHING RULES AND ADVICE THAT OUR GENERATION HAS MADE OBSOLETE

"Dress your age."

"Never wear black to a wedding."

"Wear a slip so no one can see through your dress."

"You have to suffer to be beautiful."

"Always wear a tie with a suit."

KIDS R'N'T US

I remember my mother parading in front of me in some flowered culotte outfit, asking, "Do you think this is too young for me?" How embarrassing. I knew I'd never be too old for any clothing style. But the other day I was in my favorite boutique trying on a thigh-length baby-doll dress that made me look like Edith Ann on Laugh-In. "Isn't this too young for me?" I asked my kid salesperson, who was wearing ripped jean short-shorts and a midriff-baring top. She turned away, scurried over to the counter, and brought back a handful of jewelry and belts. "Maybe you'd rather look at some accessories?" she asked. "They're on sale."

In Our Home and Car Cocoons . . . Radio and TV

As kids, we spent our time glued to transistor radios, and we are still atuned to high-frequency wavelengths as a medium.

WHAT WE LIKE ON THE RADIO NOW
- Any NPR story about a whistling convention in Idaho.
- "Adult mature" contemporary stations that play new folksy rock songs that sound like they could have been written by people when we were young or *were* written by people who were writing songs when we were young (Tracy Chapman, Edie Brickell, The Cranberries, The Rembrandts, Rickie Lee Jones, Joni Mitchell, Paul Simon, etc.).
- Lite rock and oldies stations ("The best mix of the sixties, seventies, eighties, nineties, and assorted cuts from your old album collection but without the scratches . . .").
- Sports talk shows and sex advice shows.
- Any call-in NPR show with wisecrackers telling us how to take care of our possessions ("Car Talk," "Furniture Talk," "Plumbing Talk," "Perishable Condiments Talk").

IT'S STILL
ROCK AND ROLL
TO ME

Of the old familiar triad of sex, drugs, and rock and roll, the last has changed the least. Who knew, back when "Louie, Louie" first hit the airwaves, that it would be possible thirty-five years later to be still puzzling over the lyrics nearly every day, every hour, in your car and in your kitchen?

Everyone knows that there are a lot of "oldies" frequencies—over 3,300 radio stations across the country. But what you don't know is that years ago, anticipating turf wars, the FCC carved the country into "oldies zones," specifying narrow ribbons of airspace across the country in which only one oldies hit could be played. Although you might suspect this, it is very difficult to prove unless you happen to drive across the country at just the right speed and on the right routes. To the unsuspecting few who experience it, Extreme Oldies Time Warp may seem like a nightmare.

"I didn't know what was happening," says Dwayne, a forty-three-year-old truck driver. "No matter what station I flipped on, all I could get was 'Hang on Sloopy.' " Dwayne was treated at an Oklahoma mental outpatient facility after he jumped up on the counter at a diner and began ordering Wiener schnitzel for himself as the Red Baron.

Yet even those of us who have never detected the subtle interhighway regulation of oldies have surely noticed our generation's greatest cultural contribution: emotional anachronism. It is possible to drive for hundreds of miles with a car radio on while believing that it is still 1972.

THINGS THAT ARE
NOW DANGEROUS,
OR IMMORAL ACTS
THAT WERE NORMAL
WHEN WE WERE
GROWING UP

Drinking alcohol

Smoking cigarettes

Eating veal

Serving your children Fruit Loops

Eating sunnyside-up eggs

THINGS THAT ARE COOL
NOW THAT WEREN'T COOL
TWENTY-FIVE YEARS AGO

Watching television

Country music

Sunblock

Babies

I'm Not a Grown-up,
But I Play One on TV

● ● ●

Even more important than the Nielsens in measuring boome
viewership are the BFRs (Boomer Fantasy Ratings).

Jerry Seinfeld, *Seinfeld*

Boomer Fantasy Rating (BFR) 10

On his show, Jerry has a cute apartment and a fun job as a stand
up comedian. He's still friends with his ex-girlfriend, and guys h
knows from college still drop in daily to provide witty repartee
In real life, Jerry dates eighteen-year-olds—way to go, Jer!

Candice Bergen, *Murphy Brown*

BFR 9

Nationally recognized career, post-forty fertility success, a house
painting *and* day-care professional constantly accessible in he
own home? 'Nough said.

Roseanne, *Roseanne*

BFR 6

We don't want her body, but we love her mouth. Plus she smoke
pot in her bathroom and kisses girls on the lips. In real life, she
rich and admits to having had plastic surgery.

Harry Anderson, *Night Court* reruns, *Dave's Worlc*

BFR 5

No one calls him immature when he goofs around. Wouldn't i
be fun to look boyish and do magic tricks on national television

Paul Schaefer, bandleader on *David Letterman*
BFR 7

Bald and yet still hip, he gets to sway his head back and forth while playing with just about every old rock star who's still alive.

Paul Reiser and Helen Hunt, *Mad About You*
BFR 9½

What we all want our marriages to be: filled with witty conversation, sex on the kitchen table while our friends munch hors d'oeuvres in the living room, and charming scenes with our pet dog.

Tom Skerritt and Kathy Baker, *Picket Fences*
BFR 10

He's a lot cuter and more enlightened than Andy Griffith; she has a fabulous career as a doctor; and together with their three adorable children, they solve all the town's problems each week after having a lot of heart-to-hearts in bed and over the perfect meals that seem to materialize out of thin air.

Jane Seymour, *Dr. Quinn, Medicine Woman*
BFR 5

Cute frontier dresses, nice log cabin, a respected job, adorable adopted children, and a hunk chasing after her. Your average career woman?

Homer Simpson, *The Simpsons*
BFR 0

Retro man, retro dad. How old is he supposed to be, anyway? Our worst nightmare of parenthood.

Jingles
WE'LL DREAD
HEARING

The curse of getting older is seeing the music you loved transformed into jingles for the products you now need. Here are some suggestions for future matches between songs and products.

"Whiter Shade of Pale"—Porcelana fading cream

"Time in a Bottle"—Grecian Formula

"Why Don't We Do It in the Road"—Michelin tires

"Lay Lady Lay"—Armour self-sticking bathroom tiles

"Blowin' in the Wind"—Alberto VO5 hair spray

"Fire and Rain"—Prudential insurance

"Puff the Magic Dragon"—Midol PMS formula

We Gotta Get Out of This Place:
The Vacation Thing

Okay—you were twenty-four and thought you needed a vacation. So you would drive to see your college roommate, and when you got there you'd both get drunk on Gallo Burgundy and the next day she'd decide to blow off work and you'd go out camping to a state park.

Some great time, huh?

Would you do it again?

Yeah. Maybe. If hell froze over.

Now that you're more mature, you need a real vacation: no sleeping bags, no cheap booze or food, no relatives, no *stress.*

Vacationing is getting more like exercising: it requires ever-more-elaborate programs and planning to get the relaxation fix you need. You only have two or three weeks a year in which to unwind, and you want to do it in style.

Plus, you now realize just how much it takes to drag yourself away from the job, and how much torture you will undergo when you attempt reentry. So, come to think of it, vacationing in your middle years is a lot like adultery: to be worth it, it had better be *good.*

So how do you go about choosing the right vacation for you? Fortunately, there is a whole vacation industry dedicated to making busy boomers happy, and a variety of midlife vacation genres from which to choose.

• THE VACATION EXPERIENCE •

Step 1
Consult Vacation Pornography
This includes simple brochures and newspaper ads, but the *Play boy*s of the genre are *The New York Times* travel section and glossy travel magazines such as *Travel & Leisure* and *National Geographic Traveler.* With each article you can imagine yourself in a new position on the globe, experiencing pleasure in countless ways.

Step 2
Decide on Your Destination/Experience Mode
There are a variety of midlife vacation genres from which to choose:

Merchant/Ivory jaunt: Includes all sorts of culture-laden locations such as Europe, England, and Asia. Usually involves bathroom hardships of one type or another.

Magnum P.I. pu-pu platter heaven: The mindless hit that you sometimes crave—beaches, bad rum drinks, and intimate conversations with couples you'll never see again.

Indiana Jones/Jane Goodall package: Kayaking, bicycling, making an inventory of Costa Rican katydids, climbing into oxygen-scarce zones, saving endangered mammals. Usually led by twenty-five-year-olds who also cook for you.

Family funtime: Wholesome locations with lots of fried foods, ice cream vendors, bad movies, cheap trinkets, Ferris wheels, and costumed characters.

Basketweaving 101: You always wanted to do a one-week workshop on Inuit stone-carving techniques. Or maybe your spouse always did, and you always wanted to learn to sail in a special workshop on the Chesapeake. Your friend from work is convinced that you would really enjoy his idea of a weeklong session at a "Build Your Own Dulcimer" camp in the Eastern Sierras.

Raw sex and little shampoo bottles: The weekend hotel getaway. Your parents would have called it a second honeymoon, but you're pressed for time, so it's more like a second first screw. This is the one to choose when you want to strip the vacation idea down to its basics: hot monkey love in a room where somebody cleans up after you.

Step 3
Begin Withdrawal
This is a gradual yet painful process. You must wean the people who depend daily on your work presence. Like little children, they must be told far enough in advance of your absence so that they can get used to it, and yet you can't dwell on it too much or they will get panicky.

Step 4
Liftoff!
Just don't give anyone the hotel fax number.

TUNE IN, TURN ON, WIG OUT ...
CRISIS MANAGEMENT:
A MATCHING QUIZ

When we wig out in midlife, we do it with a lot more panache than our parents, and sometimes it even leads to new career opportunities. See if you can match these crises with the New Middle Age pop figure.

1. Leave abusive husband, buzz-saw your hair, become TV exercise infomercial queen.

2. Leave supportive wife, begin eating only raw foods, talk obsessively about the ozone layer, refuse to perform for children anymore.

3. Appear in blackface and spout tasteless jokes about current girlfriend's genitalia.

4. Become obsessed with aerobics and plastic surgery, transform yourself into a fifty-year-old Barbie doll, marry communications magnate, make out with him publicly at baseball games.

5. Leave longtime girlfriend for Danish woman you meet again at your high school reunion, announce that you no longer want to be a famous radio star and will live in Denmark and write great novels, come crawling back after a few years to resume your radio show.

6. Separate from adorable younger wife, reveal in telephone conversations that you would like to become a tampon between your mistress' legs.

a. Ted Danson

b. Garrison Keillor

c. Susan Powter

d. Prince Charles

e. Jane Fonda

f. Raffi

Answers: 1. c; 2. f; 3. a; 4. e; 5. b; 6. d

Midlife Crisis Vacation Packages

THE GAUGUIN
This complete crisis getaway offers you a lush tropical setting and your own thatched hut, nubile seminude natives, and a complete change of pace. All inclusive—stay as long as twenty-five years!

THE EARHART
Disappear into a small plane to enjoy the trip of a lifetime, flying around small archipelagos in the Pacific. Includes parachute, raft, and all the roast pig you can eat. Options include becoming a native princess or double agent.

THE HUGHES
Live the high-rolling life in Las Vegas without ever leaving your fabulous hotel suite. This spa vacation will help you lose a lot of weight and monitor your bodily functions in peace and quiet. Included: all the Kleenex you need, nail polish in 165 shades, and a computerized "Write Your Own Last Will and Testament" program.

THE GARBO
The Manhattan hotel getaway taken to its ultimate: if you really want to be alone, this is the vacation package for you. Stay for the rest of your life in an obscure yet tony apartment building and enjoy the thrill of blending into crowds along Park Avenue. Large floppy hat and several pairs of sunglasses included.

Midlife's Little Instruction Book

Kissing ass is like sex: you get better at it as you get older.

Keep your Herman's Hermits obsession to yourself.

Never tell your kids how many drugs you did.

Never tell your kids how many sex partners you've had.

Go to an afternoon movie: it's cheaper than an affair.

Don't be alarmed if you occasionally see your mother or father looking back from the mirror.

If you think something looks stupid on you, it does.

Try never to use the word *awesome*.

Refrain from discussing your digestive problems on a first date.

You aren't as cute drunk as you were when you were twenty.

Don't get upset about wrinkles: they're just foreshadowing.

Some cops might look fourteen years old, but they can still give you a speeding ticket.

Your adventures with dental work and real estate seldom make good dinner party conversation.

It's never good to call your kid's teacher an "asshole."

Never compare your body to anyone else's who has a personal trainer.

Try to refrain from telling children that microwave ovens and VCRs didn't exist when you were little.

Never buy a bathing suit in the hopes that you will lose that extra ten pounds.

Getting estimates for repairs and renovations can count as a hobby.

Not everybody could do what they want for a living: How many of your close friends are ballerinas or astronauts?

Never say anything in front of your children that you don't want repeated somewhere else.

PART FOUR

Grown-up Stuff: Time, Memory, Money, Work, Etc.

Time Is on Our Side (?)

• • •

Is it just me,
or does time seem to be going faster now?

I feel like I started out on whole time, when summers stretched on endlessly. Then I moved on to 2 percent time, less satisfying, more quickly consumed. Now I'm definitely on skim time—thin, like water—and I don't like it very much. I only have time to skim books and magazine articles. What has happened?

Somewhere in Einstein's theory of time he talks about special circumstances in which time contracts. What he doesn't mention is that in very unique generations such as ours, this time contraction stuff can begin happening right after high school.

Look at your high school yearbook. You were in high school only *four years*. Yet it seemed like forever, didn't it? The sex, the Sturm und Drang, the calculus, the school plays, the drugs, the moping around, the sports, all those lab experiments and dissections—could you have possibly squeezed them into four years?

What is four years like in skim time? Nothing. At work there are people who are hired and fired in four years and you never even found out where they lived.

You have appliances you've been meaning to get repaired for four years. Diets you've been meaning to go on. The Olympics were here just four years ago and are now suddenly here again. Wasn't the presidential election just last week? If this theory scares you, take heart: time contraction can also reverse itself, and has been known to do so for groups of calendar-dependent people. Thirty, forty, or fifty years from now, you might be talkin about having lots of time on your hands. As crazy as it seems (es pecially if you are a pacifist or a vegetarian), you might star thinking of time as a beast that must be killed.

TURN, TURN, TURN

There's no reason to get obsessed by time's passage, now that we know it's all relative. Likewise with birthdays. The system we now use to measure birthdays is a geocentric, culturally bound system thought up by white male Greek astronomers thousands of years ago. You are as old as you feel. How old, really, are you? Here are some interesting new ways to measure age.

Biblical years Methusaleh lived to be 969 years old and Noah 500. So, in a biblical sense, you're still a toddler.

Dog years You're over two hundred years old in canine calculations, meaning that you've outlived the original Lassie, Rin Tin Tin, and Benji by decades.

Planetary years Say you are forty-five. On Mercury, you would be 172. Aren't you glad you live on Earth? Of course, you might choose to live on Mars, where you would only be about twenty-two. Or how about Jupiter, where you wouldn't even be three years old?

Sex years How many years have you been "doing it"? The clock, as far as we're concerned, could have started then.

Suit years In this time frame, your life as a grown-up really only began when you had to dress up for work in a suit, tie, or pantyhose. Start the age meter then.

ANNIVERSARY
D'AMOUR

I was at a New Year's Day party, reflecting on my life, when I suddenly realized that it was the twenty-fifth anniversary of the first time I had sex. It was a strange anniversary, not one I could ask people to drink to. Twenty-five years! It really freaked me out that I was old enough to have been sexually active for decades. Then I began to feel proud that I was still having sex and enjoying it. None of my other hobbies has lasted that long.

Time, time, time—see what's become of me
As I looked around for my . . . keys.

THE TIME-WASTERS
OF MIDLIFE

● ● ●

Catering to dependents   Your kids and/or your aging paren
seem to have all the time in the world, yet you're the one who has t
spend hours shopping for their running shoes, taking them to th
doctor, taking them to Chuck E. Cheese or Red Lobster, and bad
gering them about not taking drugs or taking their drugs on time.

Looking for things   Glasses, keys, can openers, scissors, con
tact lenses, forms you were supposed to fill out . . .

Personal maintenance   Jump out of bed, throw on a pair c
jeans, run out the door. Then stop and realize: I look like shi
How much more time per day is required to address the natura
changes in my face and body that seem to glare out from th
bathroom mirror each morning? That's for me to know and fo
you never to find out.

**Running into people and spending fifteen minutes talk
ing about how you're really busy but you should get to
gether some time soon**   You know you never do it.

Waiting for repairmen You have more things, and so more things are always breaking. Just keeping track of the warranty cards probably eats up five or six days a year.

Work Remember when you just went to work and then got out and lived your real life? Now work *is* real life. They expect you to be there every day and actually form sentences and sign things early in the morning. How did that happen?

THE TIME-SAVERS
OF MIDLIFE

• • •

Not bothering to spend time correcting the pronunciation or spelling of your name By now, you've seen just about every way your name can be mutilated, and unless the person is sending you a check, it just doesn't matter all that much.

Not sending holiday cards to people you don't like Ho ho ho.

Saying no You can just tell panhandlers, telephone marketers, your spouse, lover, friends, and even your boss politely but firmly that you're not interested in some offer or opportunity, and not feel crummy about it.

YOUR RANDOM ACCESS MEMORY

The human brain is often compared to a computer. Like its machine counterparts, the brain can process billions of data bytes quickly and efficiently.

The good news: Unlike its machine counterparts, the human mind will not malfunction if you spill soda on its keyboard. *The bad news:* As the brain ages, it begins to develop certain technical glitches that keep you, the end user, from gaining complete access to its database.

In your middle years, you begin to feel like you're working with an outdated unit, but the basic systems are hard-wired, so you can't upgrade. The best you can do is buy peripherals—calendars, day-planners, speed dialing, remote-control key locators, and Post-Its—to help you make the most out of the aging system you have. You can also become less frustrated when your memory experiences some downtime by learning just how the human PC really functions.

The Brain's Operating System (BOS)

This part of your brain gives basic commands that shape your life. BOS dictates what you will eat, when you will sleep, how many people you will sleep with or marry, your favorite dog breed, which way you prefer the toilet paper to hang, movie star crushes, how you eat an ear of corn, your relationship with your parents, whether you think lite beer tastes great or is less filling, how long you can stay on a stairmaster, your ability to lay floor tile, and whether you watch Leno or Letterman. This system was set in place *in utero* and cannot be altered in any way.

The Hard Disk

This contains your main database, a veritable treasure trove of information that will never leave you, no matter what. Included on the hard disk: sitcom theme songs and/or baseball stats from 1961 on; complete text and visuals from commercials for chewing gum and cleansers; the phone number you had in seventh grade; and the recipe for Chex party mix.

Also on this hard disk are bits and pieces of other data that were less successfully stored and can sometimes be reconstructed at great pain and agony by piecing together the fragments found in different sections. These include: algebra, geometry, and calculus, foreign languages, the plots of great books, how to program the VCR, the theories of Kierkegaard, the definition of DNA, and how to do comparative shopping by consulting the per-pound price tag provided by supermarket chains. Going back to school, helping with homework, watching the Discovery Channel, or taking a foreign trip can sometimes help rebuild this substantial but scrambled data network.

Floppy Disks

These loosey-goosey, flibbidigibbit components fall victim most to operator error. They are small and easy to lose as they rattle around up there. Floppy disks contain some or all of the following data: your boss's wife's name; where you put the Christmas ornaments last year; your fax number; whether you did, indeed, order a Fiberglas kayak from L.L. Bean in the middle of the night last week; the location of your keys; the combination on your lock at the gym; and the calorie count on a pint of Häagen-Dazs.

Memory

Q *There's something I wanted to ask you, but I forgot what it was.*

A That's alright. There was something I was going to tell you—I know it'll come to me if I just stop and think a minute.

Q *Oh, yeah. Here it is. Like, lately I feel stupider than I've ever felt, like I actually know **less** than I did when I was younger . . .*

A I know what you mean. But give yourself a break. It's just that you know that there's so much *out there* to know, and you know how little of it you'll ever master, and so you feel stupid. Actually, you're really smart. You know more than you ever did.

Q *Is that what you were going to tell me before?*

A No, but I'll think of it.

Q *While I have you here, who played the original Darren on Bewitched?*

A Dick York . . . or was it Dick Sargent?

At MoneyBags™, our business is (baby) booming! Cash in on our experience, and press beyond your financial plateau with one of our

Midlife One-Day Personal Finance Seminars

Can I Pay Back My Student Loans with My Social Security Checks?
Outstanding educational debts? Don't despair—learn how to strategize creatively. Along with leveraging federal stipends, the idea of "assumable" student loans for one's children will also be featured.

Coping with Moneypause
Hot flash! You're broke. Why? This supportive seminar will analyze possible reasons for your financial stress, including tuition bills, appliance overkill, the rise in the costs of a good suit, and your parents' distressing plan to live long and squander your inheritance.

Vacation Homes: Pros and Cons
This session will cover all the financial ins and outs of owning a second home. Emphasis will be placed on hidden costs, such as meals and snacks for pesky guests, replacing the coffee pot that your moron brother-in-law burned out, and extra underwear you end up buying just to keep at the other place.

Using Past Lives to Accrue Pension Years
Started your career too late? Worried that you won't be vested long enough before retirement? Learn how you can create retirement income based on past lives you have led, careers you might have held, or bank accounts you might have opened under assumed names in that other lifetime.

FINANCES:

SECRETS WE'D LIKE REVEALED

● ● ●

You're twenty. You and your friends are starting out pretty much the same. You have a spool table, Indian bed spreads, and orange crates. So do your friends. You have a VW beetle or van or an old Pinto or Opel Kadett. So do your friends. You wear jeans and T-shirts. So does every body else.

Flash forward another twenty years or so. Everybody's life is different, and you're noticing that some people your age have a lot more things than you. Nice things.

Sometimes they make more money, which could be a logical explanation. Maybe they have different spending priorities or savings patterns. (I told you not to spend so much on the Columbia Record Club!) But sometimes there doesn't seem to be any satisfactory explanation. They just have cool stuff, and you don't.

Don't you wish you could pull up next to that guy in the Jaguar and ask him how he affords it? Or that woman who looks about your age, and you're pretty sure she only has a part-time job, but she's wearing an Armani suit and definitely has a two-hundred-dollar haircut? What gives?

What we need is a financial computer program with a **REVEAL CODE** command. You could enter information about your friends and acquaintances and finally solve those mysteries that have been nagging you, like "How come he has a vacation house and I just paid off my stu dent loan?" Here's how the **REVEAL CODE** could unravel the Jaguar guy's and Armani gal's finances and make us all sleep easier:

OCCUPATION: ACCOUNTANT (DAD TOOK HIM IN, GAVE HIM A PARTNERSHIP IN SMALL FIRM)

HOUSE: $225,000 "STARTER HOME" IN NICE SUBUR-BAN NEIGHBORHOOD (GRANDMA CONVENIENTLY KICKED THE BUCKET TO PROVIDE DOWN PAYMENT)

CAR: JAGUAR (USED HIS BONUS AS DOWN PAYMENT, WIFE THREATENED TO LEAVE; HE IS SECRETLY HOP-ING TO USE A CD THAT IS ABOUT TO MATURE TO PURCHASE IT OUTRIGHT SO SHE WILL SLEEP WITH HIM AGAIN)

OCCUPATION: OWN P.R. FIRM (DOWN TO ONE CLIENT, ONLY BILLS ABOUT TEN HOURS A WEEK)

HOUSE: EXPENSIVE THREE-BEDROOM CONDOMINIUM WITH POOL AND TENNIS COURT (LIVES THERE WITH HER PARENTS; MOVED BACK IN WHEN BUSINESS BEGAN FAILING)

CLOTHES & COIFFURE: ONLY THE BEST (MASTER-CARD IS $11 AWAY FROM THE LIMIT)

Now, don't you feel better?

MIDLIFE
INSURANCE POLICIES

Worried about those special challenges of midlife? For the special needs of our generation, Regional Organic Farm Insurance Company offers:

Bimbo Protection Policy For the concerned wife who lacks a good prenuptial agreement. Continues regular payments until she finds a trophy husband of her own.

Career Disability Policy Downsizing—need we say more? This policy pays for all those extras that unemployment benefits just don't seem to cover, like dinners out, rollerblading equipment, and London theater vacations. When you've been fired, you have a lot of time on your hands to do fun things. Why screw it up by being broke?

Public Humiliation Policy Tabloid exposure or simply deep personal disgrace—either way, this policy pays up big time, allowing you to undergo extensive cosmetic surgery, fake your own death, or tap into the services of the federal Witness Protection program. You'll never have to face neighbors or coworkers again.

Rehab Policy Celebrities always seem to have that extra cash around to pay for the Betty Ford clinic, but what if *you* get caught short just when you need to go into detox?

Sports Widow Policy People used to joke about "football widows" even before the days of ESPN, Sports Channel, TNT, and ESPN2. Now one's spouse can be unavailable twenty-four hours a day as he sits channel-surfing between Bosnian bingo tournaments, Icelandic dogsledding, and the annual Girl Scout bodybuilding championships. This policy pays for an escort service for appearances at restaurants, PTA meetings, and office functions.

Sudden Weight-Gain Policy Keep up your small monthly premiums and you can pork out without fear—when you reach a weight twenty pounds over ideal, this policy will pay for a new wardrobe to buck up your spirits, send you on a spa vacation, and enroll you in a supportive weight-loss or milkshake program.

Checklist: Working Signs That You Are Officially a Grown-up

✓ You actually know how to get things done.

✓ You know when to keep your mouth shut.

✓ No one would ever refer to you as a Wunderkind.

✓ You have had more than five different business cards.

✓ Younger employees hesitate slightly before calling you by you first name.

✓ The last person you interviewed for an entry-level position re minded you of your niece.

✓ When you buy clothes, you wonder if you can wear them t work.

✓ You can never use all your vacation time.

✓ At lunch, the maitre d' seldom seats you next to the kitchen.

Career

Q *My parents think I'm strange because, at forty-four, I've already had four careers, and I'm now once again entering an entirely new field. What do you think?*

A Only four? That says "focused" to me. You forgot to say how many times you've gone back to school. If it's three or under, then you're downright conservative. Remember when you used to tell your parents that you were "finding yourself"? Just tell them now that you're finding your socioeconomic vocational niche. And tell them not to bug you again about this stuff for at least two more decades.

Q *After nearly twenty years on the job, I've decided what my problem is: I just don't like working for other people. I want to work for myself, be my own boss. Should I try it, or is this just a midlife crisis?*

A Hey, I've been there. I became my own boss over ten years ago, and let me tell you: it's not all it's cracked up to be. Think about it. All your bosses have been assholes, right? So why would you want to be your own boss and risk becoming one, too? Having yourself as a boss could lead to self-loathing. You could find yourself talking about yourself behind your back. Being my own boss didn't work out for me. I had to go out and find a regular job again after I started sexually harassing myself.

Enjoying Your Second
Adolescence

• • •

If we live to a ripe old age, we are supposed to eventually laps[e]
into a second childhood. Along the way there, during the mi[d]
dle years, do we also backslide through a second adolescence[?]
Some of us might even be in it right now. Is it different, or mor[e]
fun, than the first time around?

First Adolescence (ages thirteen to twenty-one)	Second Adolescence (ages forty to sixty)
Experiment with drugs	Experiment with drugs, bu[t] under a doctor's supervision
Worry about sex	Worry about sex
Beg parents for keys to the family car	Beg parents for keys to safe deposit box
Lie to your parents about drug use and premarital sex	Lie to your kids about drug use and premarital sex
Worry about your face (acne)	Worry about your face (acne, wrinkles, eye bags)

Experiment with hair dye	Experiment with hair dye mousse
Notice every little bodily change brought about by raging hormones	Notice every little bodily change brought about by dwindling hormones
Wonder what you're going to be when you grow up	Wonder if you'll ever grow up

---

**THE REALLY GOOD NEWS ABOUT
SECOND ADOLESCENCE**

No one can make you go to sleep at a certain time, but you usually want to, anyway.

You can play your music as loud as you want.

Car salespeople pay attention to you.

You have the money to buy better clothes.

Getting a date for the prom is no longer an issue.

You can eat pizza for breakfast and get away with it.

When Adolescence and Middle Age Merge: Some Examples

Every once in a while, some extraordinary people come along who can step right from teenhood into midlife without missing a beat.

Patti Davis: She has made hating her parents a lucrative midlife career.

Prince Charles: He has had two children, a scandalous affair, and is starting to look bad in a kilt, but he won't stop seeming like an unemployed teenager until Mommy gives up her job.

Tiny Tim: He was already long in the tooth when he started strumming that ukelele, and what could be more middle-aged than getting married on *Johnny Carson?*

Timothy Leary: By the time he started doing acid, he was at the age when short memory loss begins, so what difference did it make?

PART FIVE

Hope I Die Before I Get Old (Not!)

FUTURE SCHLOCK:

HIP PRODUCTS FOR

GRAY BOOMERS

Demographers predict that the last baby boomer will depart this earth in about 2075. We've always loved high-tech gadgets and products designed to fill our lifestyle needs. Will the last baby boomer and her friends, including us, still be ordering from those glossy catalogs?

You bet.

We won't think of ourselves as getting older, just as finding a new consumer niche. Our last decades on Earth will be just one happy string of 1-800 direct-mail opportunities.

Some gray boomer favorites around the year 2040, available on CD-ROM catalogs and the Home Shopping Network:

Cool Stuff for the Cocoon . . .

Airbag Bra/Necktie For years you have enjoyed the protection of an airbag in your car. Now you can have the same protection wherever you go, with these airbag bras and neckties that promptly inflate if you stub your toe or if your vertical orientation changes at a freefall rate. Specify size (gals) or color (guys).

AM-FM Hearing Aid—A Yawn Turns It On "Blah, blah, blah"—you've heard it all a thousand times before, and there's not enough quality time left in your life to listen to it again. So when the conversation gets excruciatingly dull, a single yawn automatically flips your hearing aid to your favorite preset AM or FM radio station. They think you're still paying attention to their tedious old tales, while you'r grooving on your music, or listening to the news.

Applesauce®   The ultimate computer for the end user. Monito your vital signs while you work and beeps when you need a nap Large keys, easy-to-read screen, fleece-lined mouse.

Bone Dry   The first Chardonnay with added calcium. (Also availab with extra estrogen and testosterone.)

Edible Book-Of-The-Month Club   These immortal classics ar bestsellers, printed in large prune-juice type on 100 percent fib paper bound with wheat gluten, *can be eaten,* page by page, as yc read them. Why clutter your short life with more objects? Why mak trips to two stores, when you can satisfy your hunger for learning ar your yearning for food at the same time? Over two hundred titles choose from in five mild flavors.

Karaoke Conversation Kit   Lip-synch along to favorite cockta party chatter. You'll never feel alone again!

Memory Memoloop   Tend to forget what you were saying? Th continuous-loop pocket tape recorder constantly records the la three minutes of your life. If you wander, don't worry; just play it bac through the cordless earphone disguised as a hearing aid, and you pick up on your thoughts almost without missing a beat.

Remote-Control Spouse Identification   Remember the emba rassment when you didn't know which was your wife at the party? (N you wouldn't, would you?) At the push of a button, her beautiful radi activated acoustical necklace will identify and locate her anywhe within a 500-foot radius. Blinking tiara version is also available for th hearing-impaired. For forgetful wives, outfit hubby with an acoustic wristwatch or blinking toupee.

Smart Mirror   A breakthrough in self-imagery! Step in front of this conventional-looking mirror and great things happen: software works immediately to remove extra weight and wrinkles, projecting a 3-D hologram of how you really want to see yourself.

The Sony Walkerman   Stereo sound and firm support in one fine light-weight aluminum unit. Earphones attach directly to each miniature speaker on the walker's legs. Detachable storage unit for CDs and medications.

Steady-Cam Torso Stabilizer   The same technology that gave you the film shots you loved now keeps you from shaking and wobbling. Available without camera or with, so you can recap the day's events.

YesterDay-Timer   Forty years ago you were concerned about what you needed to do next week. Now it is hard enough keeping track of what you did do this morning. This miracle, pocket-sized computerized life log, with built-in video camera, audio transcriber, and physical monitoring probes, keeps track of your day's activities and displays them all, at the push of a button, in easy-to-read spreadsheet form. Did you eat breakfast? Take your medicine? Talk to Mabel (a black-bordered inset gently reminds you that Mabel has been dead for twenty years)? Or you can download the day onto CD-ROM to keep a permanent record for yourself and your friends.

Moving Down Life's Highway . . .

Bifocal Car Windshield   Why didn't someone think of it before? Now you can see the pedestrian walking in front of you, read the road signs, and take in the distant view, all with a single windshield. Just send us your bifocal prescription or a spare pair of glasses, and spec ify the make, model, and year of your car. We will ship you your new windshield with easy-to-follow installation instructions.

High-Wheeler Weekend Collection   Now you can have a whee chair for all your recreational needs. Choose from our sporty single blade model, dune chair, all-terrain model, and, for that weekend i Aspen, the snomochair.

Hoovercraft   A riding vacuum cleaner for the homemaker who jus won't be stopped. Available in facsimile BMW, Cadillac, Toyota, For Taurus, and nostalgic Country Squire station wagon models.

Lincoln Incontinental   Cushioned, doughnut-shaped bucket seat with optional hide-away chamber pot for the control-impaired.

Mustang Crank-O-Matic Bed   Still yearning for that Mustang Da never bought you? Well, it may be too late for that, but here's the ne best thing. A full-feature Crank-O-Matic hospital bed in the shape that vintage car—convertible, of course. Facsimile dashboard house controls to raise or lower head and feet, at three different speed while making true-to-life engine noises. Built-in AM radio plays gen uine taped broadcasts from any year, 1962–1975 (specify), and th working horn will get anyone's attention, fast. If you can't pick up da nurses in this car, you're really lame!

Health Empowerment

Build Your Own Pacemaker   No one cares about your heart as yo do, so why should you trust it to someone else's hands? This new do it-yourself pacemaker kit enables you to custom make and impla your very own pacemaker. Buy two, and assemble one for that spe cial someone in your life—the perfect Valentine's gift. For an add tional $5, we will engrave the message of your choice—two lines, wit up to twenty-seven characters each line—on the pacemaker faceplate, so that your name or message will be engraved on your true love's heart forever. Presentation models come gift boxed and packaged with festive pink or blue 3-0 vicryl sutures.

Implosion Kit   Face it, as boomers get older, we get smaller. Our Implosion Kit includes everything you need to temporarily maintain the appearance of your original adult size until permanent arrangements can be made. Includes shoe lifts, phone books for chairs, invisible clips for temporary clothing hems, and assorted shims and extenders to bring you up, out, or otherwise closer to the things that recede from your reach.

Jet-Assisted Candle Blower   For that lung-impaired birthday boomer who still wants to get his or her wish. Developed at the Jet Propulsion Laboratory in Pasadena. Two tubes invisibly concealed in handsome reading glasses frames are connected to a backpack or IV pole–mounted natural-fuel 8-horsepower jet engine. Just the push of a button sends a candle-extinguishing 140-mph gust of clean mountain air from the Rockies in a 5-foot sweep in front of that birthday boy or girl. Large-print microprocessor lets you set the jet speed to suit the body weight and bone strength of the user.

Make Your Own Medicines   This handy kit, complete with all necessary ingredients, an illustrated step-by-step guide, empty bottles, capsules, tableting machine, etc., contains all you need to make the top 100 prescription drugs taken by gray boomers, including antihypertensives, sedatives, antipsychotics, cholesterol reducers, antiarthritics, analgesics, and more! The deluxe model includes a mini-desktop computer already loaded with RxLabelPerfect, the prescription drug label-making program, and CANDA, a Computer-Assisted New Drug Application program, so that you can create your own clinical trials and file an original 650,000-page application with the U.S. Food and Drug Administration.

UltraBones   Osteoporosis: the scourge of old age since tim[e]
began. Now nature and technology combine to banish brittle bone[s]
forever. UltraBones fools the body's normal metabolic system into in[-]
corporating a space-age graphite-titanium compound into bones an[d]
teeth instead of old-fashioned calcium. Graphite gives aging bone[s]
the flexible strength you know from high-performance tennis rac[-]
quets, while the hardness and durability of titanium, used in supe[r]
sonic military aircraft, enable you to shear childproof caps with [a]
single snap of your mighty jaws.

Your Heritage

Franklin Mint Denture Collection   Each month for twenty-eig[ht]
months you will receive one beautifully handcrafted enamel tooth[,]
each completely different and produced in a limited, numbered editio[n.]
Order now and receive, free, a set of false gums to display them in.

Tanks Full of Memories   Forgotten your life, find it too boring, [or]
just don't care, but still need to impress the grandchildren? Pick mem[-]
ories that make you the grandparent everyone wants. Kits come com[-]
plete with scripted reminiscences, artfully blended joys and sorrow[s]
together with supporting period artifacts. Send a photo, and your lik[e-]
ness will be seamlessly inserted into a lovely photograph album [to]
document your newly minted history. So thorough, so real, that whe[n]
you start getting senile you'll believe it yourself. Pick one life: *Me[n:]*
Soldier, Politician, Artist, etc. *Women:* Soldier, Politician, etc.

Final Fun

Am I Dead?   A reality home-test kit. Many gray boomers sometimes wonder whether they're really dead and just dreaming they're alive. The Am I Dead? reality check kit includes everything you need to check your continuing vitality—pocket mirror for breath detection, assorted pins to test pain response, brain-wave monitor, electrocardiogram, and on-line ObitSearch death list checking. Also includes the best-selling *100 Symptoms of Death,* compiled by a panel of the nation's leading thanatologists, medical examiners, and undertakers.

Condo Mausoleum   Ecologically and fiscally responsible boomers realize that we can't go on wasting precious irreplaceable real estate on cemeteries forever. New life-and-death Condo Mausoleums let you buy the place you want and stay forever. Live there until you die. Then your corpse or ashes are interred under the marble flooring in the foyer, behind the bathroom mirror, in the chandelier—use your imagination! For a 5 percent deduction on the purchase price, the next buyers agree to treat your resting place with dignity in perpetuity, and to admit friends and relatives to pay their respects on two pre-specified days each year.

Natural Euthanasia Kit   When the time comes to leave gracefully, do it naturally, with traditional pure organic poisons such as hemlock and asp venom. No preservatives, toxic residues, or nonbiodegradable bullets to contaminate the environment. Comes with a booklet on tasteful scenarios that will make your departure a memorable event. Also available, the Rodale guide to natural embalming using only fruit juices and spices available in any kitchen cupboard!

ObitPerfect   The latest software program from WordPerfect Corporation helps you compose your own professional obituary before you expire. An easy large-print, high-resolution tutorial takes you step-by-step through the process of writing a fascinating, dramatic, grammatically correct obituary in the standard form required by most newspapers. Order now and receive as a free bonus the fax component which guarantees immediate delivery to national newsrooms upon your demise.

Plus, don't forget the extensive
Gray Boomers Bookshelf,
featuring important titles:

Pregnancy After 80 by Demi Moore

I'm OK, But Who Am I? by Marianne Williamson

Everything You Always Wanted to Know About Your Bowels But Were Afraid to Ask by Woody Allen

The Oxford Book of Tirades Against Declining Standards edited by Michael Medved

Too Many Passages: The Rite of Incontinence by Gail Sheehy

ABOUT THE AUTHOR

Born in 1955, Cathy Crimmins has experienced almost every pleasure and humiliation a baby boomer could endure and feels a neurotic need to spill her guts about these episodes in public. She is the author of seven other books, including *YAP: The Official Young Aspiring Professional's Fast-Track Handbook* and *Curse of the Mommy: Pregnant Thoughts and Postpartum Impressions of a Reluctant Mom*. A stand-up comic, performance artist, and creator of museum exhibits and interactive software, Crimmins lives with her family in Philadelphia, the middle-aged mecca of the Western world.